WHAT ARE
SOFTSKILLS?

How to Master Essential Skills to Achieve Workplace Success

PATRICIA DORCH

Limit of Liability/Disclaimer of Warranty. The author and publisher have used their best efforts in preparing this book. This publication contains the opinions, ideas and recommendations of its author and publisher. Neither author nor publisher shall be liable for any loss of profit, or risk, personal, including but not limited to special, incidental, consequential, professional or any other commercial or other damages which is incurred as a consequence, directly or indirectly, of the use and application of any of the contents of this book. The accuracy and completeness of the information provided herein and the opinions of stated herein are not guaranteed or warranted to produce any particular results. The advice and strategies contained herein may not be suitable for every individual, organization or situation.

Dorch, Patricia

What Are Soft Skills? How to Master Essential Skills to Achieve Workplace Success/Patricia Dorch

Copyright © 2013 by Patricia Dorch, All Rights Reserved.

No part of this book may be reproduced or utilized in any means, electronic, or mechanical, including photocopying, or recording or by any information storage and retrieval system, without permission in writing from the author.

Website: www.whataresoftskills.net
Email: Patricia@whataresoftskills.net

Website: www.whatisprofessionalism.com
Email: Patricia@whatisprofessionalism.com

Website: www.jobsearchcollegegraduatesbook.com
Email: Patricia@jobsearchcollegegraduatesbook.com

Website: www.militarytociviliantransition.net
Email: Patricia@militarytociviliantransition.net

Website: www.execudress.com
Email: Patricia@execudress.com

Printed in the United States of America

ISBN – 13: 978-0-9816854-8-9
ISBN – 10: 0-9816854-8-X

DEDICATION

This book is dedicated to Willie Mae Dorch,
and
In Memory of Norman Dorch

CONTENTS

DEDICATION..3
ACKNOWLEDGEMENT...11
WHAT ARE SOFT SKILLS?...15
INTRODUCTION..15
What Are Soft Skills? The Definition.....................................15
What Are the Top Soft Skills Required in the Workplace?....15
What Types of Jobs Require Soft Skills? Can I
Learn Soft Skills on the Job?...16
Who Should Have Soft Skills?...16
Why Are Soft Skills In-Demand by Employers?.............17
Why Are Soft Skills Important to Employers?.................17
What Are the Career Benefits of Soft Skills?.....................17
Are Your Top Soft Skills Included In Your Resume and
Cover Letter?...18
Are You Looking For a Blueprint to Master Top Soft Skills?....18
Soft Skills Acronym...20

WHAT ARE SOFT SKILLS? TOP PRIMARY SOFT SKILLS

CHAPTER ONE: Adaptability...23
Adaptability: Why It Matters in the Workplace.................23
Introduction..23
What is Adaptability? The Definition.................................23
Ten Positive Characteristics of Adaptability.........................24
Ten Negative Characteristics of Adaptability.......................25
Twelve Adaptability Success Principles...............................26
Summary...29
Adaptability: Acronym..30
CHAPTER TWO: Critical Thinking Strategies....................31
Introduction..31
What is Critical Thinking? The Definition...........................31
Three Dimensions of Critical Thinking...............................32
1. Affective Strategies: How to Develop Affective Strategies..32
2. Cognitive Macro Abilities: How to Strengthen Cognitive
    Abilities...32

3. Cognitive Micro Skills: How to Develop Cognitive Skills..32
Five Smart Things A Critical Thinker Can Do.................33
A Critical Thinker Is...33
Critical Thinking Can Help You.................................33
Six Critical Thinking Strategies for Success in the Workplace...34
Summary:Critical Thinking: Key Points........................35
CHAPTER THREE: Interpersonal Communication Skills...37
Introduction...37
Ten New Strategies to Improve Interpersonal Skills.............38
Summary: Interpersonal Communication Skills: Key Points....40
CHAPTER FOUR: Diversity Communication....................41
Introduction...41
Diversity Communication: Seventeen Steps to Enhance
Diversity Communication in Today's Workplace.................42
Summary: Diversity Communication: Key Points.................44
CHAPTER FIVE: Business Communication Skills are
Vital to Success in the Workplace.............................45
Introduction...45
Job Search Communication.......................................46
Business Technology Communication............................47
Global Market Communication...................................47
Business Writing: Six Business Writing Skills Benefits...........47
Verbal Communication: Six Verbal Communication Techniques.....49
Summary: Business Communication Skills: Key Points.........49
CHAPTER SIX: Body Language.................................51
Introduction...51
Eleven Elements of Non-Verbal Communication
and Body Language..52
Five Ways to Evaluate Non-Verbal Communication Skills...54
How to Understand Non-Verbal Communication.................55
Body Language: Ten Negative Body and Language
Tips to Avoid in the Workplace...................................56
Summary: Non-Verbal Communication and Body
Language: Key Points...58
CHAPTER SEVEN: Women – The Power of Silent
Body Language..59
Introduction...59
Body Language: Ten Power and Authority Principles.............60
Summary: Women - The Power of Silent Body Language:

Key Points..62
CHAPTER EIGHT: Leadership..............................63
Leadership: Essential Leadership Skills in the
New Workplace..63
Introduction...63
Twelve New Rules of Leadership.............................64
Summary: Leadership: Key Points...........................66
CHAPTER NINE: Negotiation Skills.....................67
Effective Negotiation Skills are Critical at Work.....67
Introduction...67
What is Negotiation?...67
Six Essential Skills of Negotiators..........................68
Negotiation: Six Tips to Enhance Your Negotiation Skills....69
Summary: Negotiation Skills: Key Points................70
The Power of Salary Negotiation...........................72
Introduction...72
Visual Presentation and Perception Add Value........72
Eight Secrets of Salary Negotiation.........................73
Summary: Salary Negotiation: Key Points...............76
CHAPTER TEN: Problem Solving...........................79
Problem Solving: How to Use the PAR Formula to Solve
Problems..79
Introduction...79
THE PAR FORMULA (Problem, Action and Results)....80
Three Strategies to Problem Solve..........................80
Strategy One: Problem – Identify and Clearly Define the Problem..80
Strategy Two: Action: Develop an Action Plan.......80
Strategy Three: Results – How to Evaluate Results...................81
Summary: Problem Solving: Key Points..................81
CHAPTER ELEVEN: Professionalism.....................83
What is Professionalism? Professionalism in the Workplace...83
Introduction...83
Are You A Professional?...83
Could Your Career Be At Risk?...............................84
Do You Adhere To Company Rules?.......................84
Think Before You Hit "SEND"................................84
Sharing Too Much Information (TMI).....................85
How Do You Look?...85
Seventeen Top Characteristics of a Professional Employee....85

Thirteen "Red Flag" Traits of an Unprofessional Employee....86
Summary: Professionalism: Key Points.................................87
CHAPTER TWELVE: Personal Accountability..................89
Personal Accountability: How to Be Accountable.................89
Introduction...89
Twenty Personal Accountability Principles............................89
Summary: Personal Accountability: Key Points....................92
Accountability Acronym..94
CHAPTER THIRTEEN: Teamwork Accountability.........95
Teamwork Accountability Qualities.......................................95
Introduction...95
Five Teamwork Accountability Qualities...............................96
How Do You Perform As A Team Leader?............................97
Summary: Teamwork Accountability: Key Points.................97

WHAT ARE SOFT SKILLS? TOP SECONDARY SOFT SKILLS

CHAPTER FOURTEEN: Decision Making......................101
Effective Decision Making...101
Introduction...101
Five Types of Decision Making for Complex Issues..........102
The Decision Making Process Critical Steps of
Making a Good Decision..102
Six Critical Steps of Decision Making................................102
Leadership Decision Making: Six Steps of
Leadership Decision Making..103
Summary: Effective Decision Making: Key Points.............104
CHAPTER FIFTEEN: Enthusiasm...............................105
Enthusiasm: The Key to a Successful Future.......................105
Introduction...105
How Do You Develop Enthusiasm? Six Ways
to Develop Enthusiasm..106
What Are the Benefits of Enthusiasm? Ten Benefits
of Enthusiasm..107
Summary: Enthusiasm: Key Points......................................108
CHAPTER SIXTEEN: Integrity.................................111
Integrity for Today's Workplace..111
Introduction...111
Eleven Integrity Characteristics for Success........................111

Ten Integrity Success Principles.............................112
Summary: Integrity: Key Points.............................114
CHAPTER SEVENTEEN: Listening...............................115
Power of Listening.............................115
Introduction.............................115
Five Reasons Listening is Important.............................116
Active Listening: Fifteen New Techniques
for Active Listening.............................116
Active Listener: Seventeen Team Member Strategies
for Active Listening.............................118
Strategic Listening: Four Levels of Strategic Listening......122
Summary: The Power of Listening: Key Points.............124
CHAPTER EIGHTEEN: People Skills...............................125
Build Your People Skills: How to Succeed at Work.............125
Introduction.............................125
Twenty One Strategies to Improve People Skills.............126
Summary: People Skills: Key Points.............................128
CHAPTER NINETEEN: Public Speaking...............................131
Master the Benefits of Public Speaking: Speak for Success......131
Introduction.............................131
Fifteen Benefits to Speak for Success.............................133
Summary : Public Speaking: Key Points.............................134
CHAPTER TWENTY: Risk Taking...............................135
Are You A Risk Taker? How to Take Risks and Get
Ahead at Work.............................135
Introduction.............................135
Three Types of Risks Probability.............................135
Risk Management: Seven Ways to Manage Risks.............136
Risk Taking: Six Types of Risk Taking to Avoid.............137
Risk Taking: Five Benefits to Risk Taking.............................138
Summary: Risk Taking: Key Points.............................139
CHAPTER TWENTY ONE: Self Confidence...............................141
Self Confidence: Thirteen Steps to Build Self Confidence.......141
Introduction.............................141
Thirteen Steps to Build Self Confidence.............................142
Summary: Self Confidence: Key Points.............................144
CHAPTER TWENTY TWO: Self Motivation...............................147
Self Motivation: Motivate Yourself to Accomplish Goals.....147
Introduction.............................147

Eleven Smart Tips to Get Motivated..................................147
Summary: Self Motivation: Key Points..............................149
CHAPTER TWENTY THREE: Time Management..........151
Time Management: How to Increase Workplace Productivity.......
Introduction..151
Fourteen Tools to Help You Be Productive.........................152
Summary: Time Management: Key Points.........................155
CHAPTER TWENTY FOUR: How To Network...............157
How To Network: Seventeen Essential Business Strategies
for the 21st Century..157
Introduction..157
How to N.E.T.W.O.R.K Acronym....................................158
Strategy 1: Introductions and Marketing Statement
("Elevator Speech")..159
Strategy 2: Business Image Tips..161
Strategy 3: How to Define Your Networking Goals.............162
Strategy 4: Information, Influence, Resources and Volunteer.........163
Strategy 5: How to Exchange Business Cards.....................164
Strategy 6: How to Manage Your Contacts.........................166
Strategy 7: How to Make Small Conversations...................167
Strategy 8: How to Engage Your Connection.....................168
Strategy 9: How to Close the Conversation.......................169
Strategy 10: How to Listen..170
Strategy 11: How to Work the Room.................................170
Strategy 12: How to Build Trust..171
Strategy 13: Power Etiquette and Manners.......................172
Strategy 14: How to Follow-Up...173
Strategy 15: How to Network at Work...............................174
Strategy 16: Networking Organizations.............................176
Strategy 17: How to Network as a Way of Life...................177
Summary...177
CHAPTER TWENTY FIVE: Technology.......................179
Technology Skills..179

SOFT SKILLS ACRONYM..180
Summary: What Are Soft Skills? How to Master
Essential Skills to Achieve Workplace Success.......................181
ABOUT THE AUTHOR...182
Professional and Job Search Resources............................185

ACKNOWLEDGEMENT

I want to extend my personal and sincere thanks to all who have dedicated their time, expertise and advice for this book. Your knowledge and support have contributed to my success.

"Soft skills enhance your marketability for career success."

-PATRICIA DORCH

"Soft skills enhance your marketability
for career success."
-PATRICIA DORCH

WHAT ARE
SOFT**SKILLS?**

How to Master Essential Skills to Achieve
Workplace Success

INTRODUCTION

Do You Have the Top Soft Skills
In-Demand by Employers?

What Are Soft Skills? The Definition

Soft skills are your interpersonal skills, personality and character traits, and social skills. They are transferable from one occupation to another, whereas hard skills are measurable abilities you have acquired which are job specific.

What Are the Top Soft Skills Required in the Workplace?

Soft skills are the secret to finding work. Although soft skills can vary based on the job description, employers seek candidates who have communication skills, listening skills, adaptability, interpersonal communication skills, leadership skills, teamwork, critical thinking skills, negotiation skills, a strong work ethic and other important soft skills.

What Types of Jobs Require Soft Skills? Can I Learn Soft Skills on the Job?

No matter what your college major or profession – you need soft skills to get hired, promoted and maintain your employment.

Each employer's job description provides a list of soft skills required for employment. There are primary and secondary employability soft skills. Employers spend less time providing "traditional training" of core competency skills – therefore you are expected to take *ownership, be accountable* and *responsible* for your professional development skills essential to employment. Although most employers have internal online universities to enhance your skills – you are expected to have the required soft skills to be successful.

Who Should Have Soft Skills?

Professionals who should have soft skills include:
- Career Colleges – Non-Technical and Technical
- College Graduates
- College Students
- Entrepreneurs
- International Graduates
- International Students
- Interns
- Leadership Programs

- Mentoring Programs
- Military To Civilian Transition Programs
- Professionalism Programs
- Professionals – Experience and Inexperienced
- Workers Returning to the Workforce

Why Are Soft Skills In-Demand by Employers?

Employers seek candidates who have soft skills which allow you to adapt to workplace situations, and determine how you will interact with management, coworkers, customers and clients. Business skills play a crucial role in employment and the reason why they are sought after by employers. Soft skills can open or close a door for a new career or promotion.

Why Are Soft Skills Important to Employers?

Soft skills are the underlying principles of a company's professionalism and essential to your career success – in building long-term strategic relationships with customers and clients for profitable results.

What Are the Career Benefits of Soft Skills?

The long-term career benefits of soft skills in your skill portfolio will elevate you above the competition; make you more marketable, visible, productive and successful at work. Soft skills are essential to effectively interact with others in the workplace and social settings. Soft skills will define you as a person and convey a lasting impression to management, co-workers and others about you.

Did You Know?

- *Adaptable* – *Employers seek employees who are adaptable and can adjust to the work environment, new ideas and work habits.*
- *Critical Thinking* – *Critical thinking requires your ability to use facts; knowledge and data to problem solve to achieve desired results.*
- *Interpersonal Communication* – *Interpersonal skills are important to get hired and be successful in any job.*
- *Leadership* – *Leadership skills empower you to lead instead of manage a team.*
- *Public Speaking* – *Public speaking is a skill every professional should possess.*
- *Teamwork* – *Every job requires you to interact for business and social reasons which is why teamwork is important.*

Are Your Top Soft Skills Included In Your Resume and Cover Letter?

Employers hire and promote employees who have employability skills; therefore they should be included in your resume and cover letter in addition to hard skills based on the job description. During your interview an employer may ask you to describe how you used a specific soft skill in current or past employment, internships or volunteer work. You will need to effectively communicate how you used soft skills to achieve specific organizational goals.

Are You Looking For a Blueprint to Master Top Soft Skills?

*Inside **What Are Soft Skills? How to Master Essential Skills to Achieve Workplace Success*** you will learn how to master essential employability soft skills – use secret strategies, techniques, tips and tools to boost your knowledge, professionalism and increase your marketability.

What Are Soft Skills? is a comprehensive career resource which will enable you to develop and enhance top employability skills required by employers. Employability skills are your knowledge, skills and abilities – and how you communicate your marketable skills to employers to get hired.

"Soft skills enhance your marketability for career success."

-PATRICIA DORCH

SOFT SKILLS FOR CAREER SUCCESS

Soft skills are essential for employment, management and leadership positions.

Oral and written communication skills are important to get hired and promoted.

Flexibility allows you to easily adapt to the work environment, new ideas and work habits.

Teamwork requires active participants who listen, speak up, and take the initiative to make things happen.

Strong work ethic is critical to achieve organizational goals.

Knowledge is needed to perform the required tasks in the workplace.

Interpersonal communication skills are essential in every area of your life.

Listening skills increases your ability to influence, increase productivity, effectively negotiate and reduce misunderstandings.

Leadership skills empower you to lead instead of manage your team.

Speaking skills builds self confidence and increases your value in the workplace.

WHAT ARE
SOFT**SKILLS**?

TOP PRIMARY SOFT SKILLS

"Change is certain – embrace it."
- PATRICIA DORCH

CHAPTER ONE

ADAPTABILITY

Adaptability:
Why It Matters In The Workplace

INTRODUCTION

Are you adaptable? Can you adapt to the new demands of the changing workplace and personal behaviors of others?

What is Adaptability? The Definition

Adaptability is being open to changing and changed situations in business and social settings. A person who adapts is able to learn new information regardless of your current skills or preconceived judgments although it may be uncomfortable. Adaptability improves your ability to compete professionally.

Employers seek employees who can easily adapt to the work environment, new ideas, technology, work habits, techniques and strategies. Adaptability affects internal and external business relationships, contributions, performance, growth and financial results.

Ten Positive Characteristics of Adaptability

Listed are ten positive characteristics of adaptability to effectively communicate, be productive and build strategic relationships.

1. Confidence
- Believe in yourself.
- Trust your instincts and judgment.

2. Tolerance
- Be open and accept opinions and processes that may be different than your own.

3. Empathy
- Acknowledge others feelings of joy and pain.

4. Be Positive
- Demonstrate a positive attitude in everything you do.

5. Respect Others
- Have a sincere desire to understand and respect others choices, differences and needs.

6. Resilience
- Know how to overcome barriers, and setbacks.
- Have an attitude to succeed regardless of obstacles you may encounter.

7. Vision
- Be creative.
- Have an imagination.
- Determine alternatives.

8. Attentive
- Be aware of your environment and how people react.
- Know when or when not to act.
- Determine the right time to present ideas or wait for another opportunity.

9. Competence
- The ability to problem solve and determine who could best resolve a situation.
- Have a can do attitude.
- Follow-up and follow through to solve the problem.

10. Self Correction
- Ask for feedback regarding a project.
- Set a high priority to problem solve.
- Know when – what you are doing is not working and identify alternative strategies.

Listed are ten negative characteristics of adaptability to avoid in the workplace.

Ten Negative Characteristics of Adaptability

1. **Blunt** - "That's stupid."
2. **Competition** - Competes with others – "I'm more intelligent than you are" – "I look better than you do?
3. **ME** - Single Mindedness – "It's all about me."
4. **My Way** – "Why can't I have it my way?"

5. **Now** – Let's do it NOW.
6. **Resistance** – "We have always done it this way."
7. **Rigid** – "I want it my way."
8. **Risk** - Takes unreasonable risks.
9. **Subjective** – "This is how it works for ME."
10. **Unapproachable** – Has no social skills – "Unless you see it my way – don't bother me."

Twelve Adaptability Success Principles

In the workplace use adaptive success principles to build skills, gain industry knowledge to achieve organizational goals. Listed are twelve adaptability success principles.

Success Principle One: Comfort Zone
- Adaptability is a skill required to be successful in the workplace.
- Adapt to a new environment.

Success Principle Two: Company Culture
- Adapt and anticipate day to day changes.
- Adapt your work style to the company culture.
- Adapt to the company's mission, goals, values and expectations.

Success Principle Three: Company Image
- Executive level positions require you adapt and immediately embrace the company image.
- A personality match will enhance your success.

Success Principle Four: Creative Thinking
- Use creative thinking to solve new complex problems.

Success Principle Five: Cultural and Environment Adaptability

- Adapt to different cultures.
- Adapt to internal language and acronyms unique to the company.
- Be aware of written and unwritten rules, policies and procedures.
- Adapt to a new environment.
- Understand expectations for accepted values, rules, customs and guidelines.

Success Principle Six: Industry Change

- Keep pace with industry changes.
- Stay on top of new products, services, research, competitors and techniques.
- Subscribe to industry newsletters – share industry news with management and co-workers.

Success Principle Seven: Interpersonal Relationships

- Adapt your behavior to effectively communicate with management, executives, co-workers and customers.
- Demonstrate your flexibility to achieve organizational goals.
- Adapt to internal and external needs to improve interpersonal relationships.

Success Principle Eight: New Challenges

- New work challenges enhance your skills.
- New challenges lead to career growth and success.
- New challenges can open the door to new and improved relationships and career opportunities.
- Embrace challenges others avoid.
- Be open to new challenges regardless of your skills.

Success Principle Nine: Physical Adaptability
- Adapt to physical factors such as location, climate, and noise level – depending on the job description.

Success Principle Ten: Strive for Excellence
- Research an industry topic on the internet to broaden your industry knowledge.
- Read books to gain industry knowledge.
- Write an article and post it on article submission websites to be seen as an industry expert.
- Always strive for excellence – self improvement.

Success Principle Eleven: Procedures, Tasks and Technologies
- Adapt to new and improved tasks.
- Adapt to and anticipate future needs by learning new tasks, technologies and procedures.
- Adapt to the importance of continuous learning as an ongoing process.

Success Principle Twelve: Work Situations
- Adapt to organizational restructuring.
- Adapt to new business priorities.
- Adapt your focus when necessary.
- Adapt to work situations that include reductions and new changes.

Summary

Adaptability

Key Points:
- Adaptable people easily adjust to their environment, work habits, technology, techniques and strategies that affects performance in the workplace.
- Adapt to new challenges regardless of your skills.
- Adaptability leads to career growth and improved relationships.
- Adapt to external change in your industry.
- Adapt your focus to current work situations.
- Adapt and demonstrate a positive attitude in everything you do.

ADAPTABILITY

Adaptability is ranked as one of the top skills employers look for in job candidates.

Day to day changes requires the ability to adapt to company expectations.

Adapt to new challenges and initiatives associated with downsizing and reengineering to improve productivity.

People who are adaptable are flexible and versatile.

Technical innovation requires continuous learning in the workplace.

Adapt to job requirements by learning new roles, procedures, tasks and technologies.

Be positive about everything you do.

Interpersonal relationships allow you to effectively adapt and communicate to others.

Lack of a willingness to adapt to a new environment can limit career success.

Industry changes require you to stay on top of new products, services, technologies and competitors.

Tolerance is required for opinions and processes that may be different than your own.

You are expected to adapt to internal language and acronyms unique to the company.

CHAPTER TWO

CRITICAL THINKING

Critical Thinking Strategies
How To Enhance Your Creativity

INTRODUCTION

Are you a critical thinker? Do you have critical thinking skills to be effective and marketable in the workplace? Do you know what it takes to improve your critical thinking?
Critical thinking skills help college students and professionals increase performance – academically and professionally. These skills help you learn about your abilities, how you interact with people and process information.

What is Critical Thinking? The Definition

Critical thinking involves analyzing, communication, problem-solving and reasoning. Use critical thinking skills to gather facts required to get to the truth. A critical thinker is one who can think clearly and be an independent thinker. Critical thinking is a powerful and important skill to possess in a fast pace and changing workplace.

Three Dimensions of Critical Thinking

There are three dimensions of critical thinking – Affective Strategies, Cognitive Strategies – Macro Abilities and Cognitive Strategies – Micro Skills.

Dimension One: Affective Strategies: How to Develop Affective Strategies
- Think independently.
- Develop self confidence.
- Develop courage.
- Learn about multiple topics to gain intellectual knowledge.

Dimension Two – Cognitive Strategies – Macro Abilities: How to Strengthen Cognitive Abilities
- Learn how to evaluate the credibility of information.
- Learn how to analyze information based on knowledge you currently have.

Dimension Three: Cognitive Strategies – Micro Skills: How to Develop Cognitive Skills
- Focus on specific information.
- Recognize contradictions.
- Distinguish between relevant and irrelevant information.
- Evaluate information provided.
- Learn to determine the facts or evidence provided supports the arguments.

Five Smart Things A Critical Thinker Can Do

A Critical Thinker Should Be Able To:

1. Identify common mistakes and reasoning.
2. Identify the importance of ideas.
3. Understand the connections between ideas.
4. Problem solve – identify problems and solve them systematically.
5. Use one's own beliefs and value systems in the thinking process.

What Is A Critical Thinker

A Critical Thinker Is:
1. Adaptable
2. Fair minded
3. Inquisitive
4. Open minded
5. Reasonable
6. Seeks relevant information to make decisions
7. Seeks results

Critical Thinking Can Help You:
1. Acquire knowledge
2. Improve and enhance theories
3. Strengthen disagreements
4. Enhance work processes
5. Improve the workplace
6. Improve your comprehension ability
7. Enhances presentation skills
8. Improve creativity

9. Improve self-evaluation
10. Express new ideas – express, modify and implement new ideas

Critical Thinking Strategies for Success in the Workplace

Six Critical Thinking Strategies

Strategy One: Trends
- Learn new ideas and trends in your industry.

Strategy Two: Industry Changes
- Gain insight how changes affect your organization and industry.

Strategy Three: Ask Questions
- Ask questions to problem solve: - Who, What, When Where, Why and How.

Strategy Four: Think Differently
- Challenge yourself and those you work with to think differently.

Strategy Five: Read
- Read books, magazines, newsletters, blogs and search the internet for current topics.

Strategy Six: Problem Solve
- Seek new opinions from co-workers to trigger creativity and new innovative approaches to problem solve.

Summary

Critical Thinking

Key Points:

- There are three dimensions of critical thinking – affective strategies, cognitive strategies – macro skills, cognitive strategies – micro skills.
- A critical thinker thinks clearly and is an independent thinker.
- Problem solves systematically.
- Seeks relevant information to make decisions.
- Critical thinking can improve your comprehension.
- Critical thinking skills enhance your creativity.
- There are six critical thinking strategies for success in the workplace.

CHAPTER THREE

INTERPERSONAL COMMUNICATION

Interpersonal Communication Skills
Ten New Strategies to Improve Communication

INTRODUCTION

Can you connect and get along with your colleagues in the workplace? Are you comfortable talking to people you do not know?

Interpersonal skills in the workplace are vital to your career success to gain employment and get promoted. Employers expect you have the ability to interact with people of different personalities and cultures – therefore it's important to acquire interpersonal skills to be successful at work. Interpersonal skills are the key ingredient in communication skills. Listed are new strategies to improve your interpersonal skills.

Ten New Strategies to Improve Interpersonal Skills

Strategy One: Be Positive
- Be friendly to everyone.
- Maintain a positive upbeat attitude at all times.
- Smile and draw others to you.

Strategy Two: Be Appreciative
- Focus on those things that are positive.
- Praise others.
- Be supportive and encourage others.
- Say 'thank you" for compliments and when others help you.

Strategy Three: Be Observant
- Acknowledge what is going on around you.
- Make positive eye contact and address others by the name they prefer to be called.

Strategy Four: Active Listening
- Actively listen to others.
- Be aware of your body language to show you care about what is being said.
- Listen to understand another person's perspective.
- Confirm your understanding by restating what was said in your own words.

Strategy Five: Treat Everyone Equally
- Do not talk about others behind their back – keep your comments to yourself.
- Confirm you are understood when you present an idea or announcement.

Strategy Six: Resolve Conflicts
- Be seen as a person who can resolve conflicts.
- Be an effective negotiator.
- Resolving conflicts will position you as a leader to gain the respect of others.

Strategy Seven: Clear Communication
- What you say is as important as how you say it.
- Clear effective communication helps to avoid misunderstandings.
- Think before you speak – to gain the respect of others.
- Speak clearly and confidently.

Strategy Eight: Be Happy
- Humor is an effective tool to overcome barriers and gain acceptance.
- A little humor goes a long way.

Strategy Nine: Empathy
- See things from another person's perspective.
- Stay in touch with your own emotions.

Strategy Ten: Do Not Complain
- Avoid a bad reputation by not complaining to management, co-workers and associates.
- If you must vent – do so to those outside of the workplace.

Summary

Interpersonal Communication Skills

Key Points:
- The ability to connect with people in the workplace will enable you to have a successful career.
- Interpersonal communication skills allow you to become more effective and respected in the workplace.
- The key ingredient in interacting with others is great interpersonal communication skills.
- The ability to get along with others requires interpersonal skills.
- Interpersonal communication strategies help you improve your communication skills.

CHAPTER FOUR

DIVERSITY COMMUNICATION

Diversity Communication
How to Enhance Communication Competence

INTRODUCTION

How well do you communicate with other cultures? Do you need to improve your diversity competence?

Employers expect you have the ability to effectively interact with others in a diverse workplace. To increase productivity in the workplace and close the achievement gap each employee is accountable for multicultural communication knowledge and skills. These essential skills are required to embrace and celebrate a diverse work environment. Diversity communication competence will empower you to effectively communicate with others. Listed are steps to embrace diversity, productivity and marketable skills.

Diversity Communication: Seventeen Steps to Enhance Diversity Communication in Today's Workplace

Step One: Misunderstandings
- Expect misunderstandings will sometimes occur.
- Remain calm and address the situation with the appropriate persons.

Step Two: Do Not Assume
- Although your intentions may be good – do not make assumptions when dealing with other cultures.

Step Three: Ask for Information
- When a problem is identified ask for information that will help you solve the problem.

Step Four: Individual and Cultural Differences
- Ask questions to learn about different cultural values and differences.

Step Five: Do Not Generalize
- Do not generalize about a particular culture or individual.

Step Six: Confirm Understanding
- When you are unsure about what has been said – ask for clarification to confirm your understanding.

Step Seven: Decision Making
- Include other cultures in discussions and the decision making process.

Step Eight: Adapt to Communication Styles
- Adapt your communication style to the individual culture and situation.

Step Nine: Take Responsibility

- Take responsibility for interpersonal successes and those that may be challenging.
- Learn from your experiences.

Step Ten: Hot Button Topics

- Avoid "hot button" topics such as inappropriate language, touching, ethnic jokes and racial assumptions that may cause others to be offended and uncomfortable.

Step Eleven: Good Will

- Work together as a spirit of good will and trust of others.

Step Twelve: Conflict

- Determine if your communication style is the reason for the conflict instead of the individual and culture.

Step Thirteen: Behavior

- Do not be distracted by a person's accent, appearance, style, tone, disability, grammar – rather focus on their behavior and how they communicate.

Step Fourteen: Feedback

- Provide honest and open feedback – however do not be disrespectable.

Step Fifteen: Non-Verbal Communication

- Be aware of your non-verbal communication when you interact with others.

Step Sixteen: New Relationships

- Be open and seek out new relationships with people of different cultures.

Step Seventeen: Trust
- Trust is earned.
- Do not expect someone to immediately trust you.
- There are different levels of trust based on individual relationships.

Summary

Diversity Communication

Key Points:
- Diversity competence is essential to your success in the workplace.
- Closing the diversity skills gap will increase workplace productivity.
- Ask questions to learn and respect cultural differences and values.
- Take responsibility for interpersonal successes and challenges.
- Trust is earned. Do not expect someone to immediately trust you – build trust over time.

CHAPTER FIVE

BUSINESS COMMUNICATION

**Business Communication Skills are
Vital to Career Success in the Workplace**

INTRODUCTION

**How well does your oral and written communication
measure up in the workplace? Do you communicate well in
writing and verbal communication?**

Writing is the essential means of communication in the workplace. Writing is an important business communication tool which allows you to express your ideas, thoughts and views to others to be productive.

Today's competitive work environment requires good communication skills at all levels of the organization and the essential component to career success. Whether you communicate to a single individual, face to face conversations, a group of people or by email it requires good communication skills.

Can you communicate effectively?

The ability to effectively communicate will enable you to adapt to the changing work environment. Employers seek employees who can communicate their thoughts in verbal and written communication. Successful communication skills are important to:

1. Interview
- To secure an interview and complete the application requirements.

2. Get Hired
- You need good communication skills to sell yourself to gain the job offer.

3. Performance
- Good communication skills impact your performance and productivity in the workplace.

Job Search Communication

Are you looking for a job or seeking a promotion?

Only the most well spoken candidates make the best impression and capture the attention of the hiring team. To get your foot in the door you need to communicate effectively in written and verbal communication. Your first written communication is your resume and cover letter. Once you have a telephone or face to face interview you must verbally communicate your knowledge, skills and abilities and why you are the best candidate for the job.

Business Technology Communication

Could your career be at risk?

Current business technologies such as the internet and voicemail are necessary tools which require you to write, spell and communicate verbally. The lack of good communication skills such as spelling errors, poor grammar take away from your message, professionalism and limit your chances of career advancement.

Global Market Communication

Do you take short cuts when you communicate in writing?

The global market and new diverse workplace emphasizes good communication skills with all people. The use of technology requires good communication with internal, external customers and those around the globe. Language barriers and cultural differences require the use of direct communication skills free of humor and symbols that are not universal to avoid misunderstanding especially in written communication. Listed are benefits of business writing skills in the workplace.

Business Writing: Six Business Writing Skills Benefits:

1. Clarity
- Express clearly on paper what your mean.

2. Confidence
- Expressing yourself well in writing conveys confidence.

3. Completeness
- Completely express your point to avoid misunderstanding and unnecessary questions.

4. Persuasion
- Sales and marketing professionals use persuasion to gain confidence of clients and customers to purchase products and services.
- Internal customers use persuasion to communicate to gain acceptance of their thoughts and ideas to peers and management.

5. Professionalism
- Written communication includes well written sentences, spell and grammar check.
- Do not rely entirely on electronic grammar check – take a few minutes to read what you have written to ensure you have the correct words to convey your message.

6. Team Building
- Team building allows executives and management to communicate in writing company mission, vision, goals, changes, products, services and accomplishments.

Verbal Communication

One of the most important things you can do in communication is to keep your message simple, clear and to the point. Listed are effective techniques to communicate your verbal message.

Six Verbal Communication Techniques

Technique One: Organize Your Thoughts
- Organize your thoughts.
- Think before you speak.

Technique Two: Say What You Mean
- Say exactly what you mean to say – always be professional.

Technique Three: Make Your Point
- Make your point – do not lose your audience.
- Use good judgment.

Technique Four: Be Brief
- Speak plainly and briefly – do not go on and on.

Technique Five: Be Yourself
- Be yourself and let your personality shine through you.

Technique Six: Speak in Images
- Use words that help people visualize your message.

Summary

Business Communication Skills

Key Points:
- You need good communication skills to get hired and promoted.
- Current technologies require you to write, spell and communicate effectively.

- Verbal communication requires you keep your message simple and clear.
- In the global market language barriers and cultural differences require direct communication to avoid misunderstandings.
- Communicating well in writing conveys confidence.

CHAPTER SIX

BODY LANGUAGE

Body Language
The Power of Non-Verbal Communication

INTRODUCTION

What does your body language communicate to an employer and others about you?

We interact at work and personally in both verbal and non-verbal communication. Communication is vital to success in the workplace – behaviors such as the way we look, talk, distance you stand from others communicate non-verbal signals such as:

- Understanding
- Confusion
- Interest
- Trust
- Respect

Non-verbal communication is a powerful tool used to build relationships by connecting with other people. The way in which people respond to your body language indicates whether they are in agreement or not in what you are communicating. Non-verbal communication is eye contact, facial expressions, gestures, posture and tone of voice when you communicate with others.

In the workplace non-verbal communication speaks volumes about you – it communicates your interest in others. Listed are elements of non-verbal communication and body language.

Eleven Elements of Non-Verbal Communication and Body Language

Element One: Body Movements
- What does your body movements communicate to others about you?
- Your body speaks louder than your words.
- The way you sit, walk, use your hands, or hold your head communicates a wealth of information about you.

Element Two: Eye Contact
- Eye contact is critical in communicating to others your interest, affection, attraction or hostility.
- Eye contact helps you gauge another person's response.

Element Three: Facial Expression
- Facial expressions communicate emotions.
- Facial expressions are universal for happiness, surprise, fear, anger and disgust.

Element Four: Gestures
- Gestures communicate different things across different cultures.
- Be conscious what your gestures communicate to others.
- Be aware to communicate what you want to say.

Element Five: Office Cubicle – Cubicle Appearance
- What does your office or cubicle space communicate to others about you?
- A cluttered desk or work area gives the appearance you are not organized.
- An uncluttered work area indicates you are organized and know what you are doing.

Element Six: Physical Space
- Are you comfortable when someone is standing too close to you?
- Your comfort level will depend on the relationship you have with the person you are communicating with.

Element Seven: Posture
- Be conscious of your posture, stance and movements.
- Sit up straight.
- Do not slouch.
- Leaning slightly forward indicates to the speaker you are interested in what they are communicating.

Element Eight: Time
- Respect management and your co-workers time.
- Being on time for meetings and teleconferences is vital to your success.
- Being late indicates a lack of respect, professionalism and importance of others time and will not go unnoticed.

Element Nine: Touch
- People communicate through touch – the way they shake your hand, touch you on the arm or embrace you.

Element Ten: Vocal Tone
- The tone and pitch of your voice is important when you speak.
- What you say is equally as important as the tone which you say it.
- Your tone communicates important cues such as confidence, sarcasm and others when you speak.

Element Eleven: Relationships – Non-Verbal Communication and Body Language
- Non-verbal communications skills help improve relationships.
- Ability to read people and unspoken messages.
- Create trust based on non-verbal signals.
- Respond with non-verbal cues that communicate interest and understanding.

Five Ways to Evaluate Non-Verbal Communication Skills

One: Eye Contact
- Do I give direct eye contact to the person who is speaking to me?

Two: Facial Expression
- Does my social expression communicate my interest or emotion?

Three: Vocal Tone
- Does my voice communicate confidence, happiness, anger, resentment, or disappointment?

Four: Posture and Gesture
- What does my posture say about me?
- Is my body relaxed or tensed?
- Are my gestures appropriate for my communication?

Five: Touch
- How do I respond when someone touches me?
- Do I prefer not to be touched?

How to Understand Non-Verbal Communication

Can you read non-verbal communication?
No matter what your position is in the workplace the ability to read non-verbal communication will improve with practice. Recognize the power of non-verbal communication and pay attention to non-verbal cues. Listed are tips to help you understand the importance and value of non-verbal communication.

Four Tips to Understand Non-Verbal Communication

Tip One: Listen to Non-Verbal Communication
- If what a person is saying is different from their non-verbal communication – listen to the non-verbal communication.

Tip Two: Interview Non-Verbal Communication
- Job candidates are evaluated based on non-verbal communication.
- Non-verbal communication during an interview can indicate a candidate's skills, strengths or weaknesses.

Tip Three: Probe – Non-Verbal Communication
- Probe to gather information and get the facts.
- You may discover non-verbal communication may uncover more than spoken words.

Tip Four: Recognize Non-Verbal Communication Cues
- When someone wants to speak.
- When the mood of the audience changes.
- When you have lost your audience in what you are communicating.
- When you have talked too long.

Body Language: Ten Negative Body and Language Tips to Avoid in the Workplace

Tip 1: Rolling Your Eyes. Rolling your eyes at your supervisor, manager or your peers.

Tip 2: Clenching Fists. Communicates you are experiencing tension or anxiety.

Tip 3: Arms. Arms crossed over your chest can be viewed as defensive.

Tip 4: Neck Movements. Neck movements shows lack of controlled behavior and inappropriate in the workplace.

Tip 5: Hand Movements. Finger snapping and arm movements. Unprofessional and inappropriate in any situation.

Tip 6: Hands on Hips. This can translate – "I'm not in agreement with what you are saying" or "Do not tell me what to do."

Tip 7: Touching Others. Touching others although the intention may be friendly could be misinterpreted. If you touch another person observe their reaction to see how your physical contact affects them. You might consider asking them how they feel when you touch them or perhaps not touch at all. *Never* touch someone when they are upset.

Tip 8. Barriers. Crossing your arms or standing behind a desk or chair.

Tip 9: Unprofessional Language. The use of unprofessional language in the workplace such shows your lack of ability to effectively communicate in a professional manner.

Tip 10: Unprofessional Word – The use of the word "freaking" is interpreted as the "f" curse word.

The "f" word is frequently used by some age groups with their peers as common language in a social environment which tends to carry over in the workplace. Using any form of the "f" word shows a lack of communication skills, emotional control and professionalism. Using the "f" word is a career limiting choice.

Summary

Non-Verbal Communication and Body Language

Key Points:
- In the workplace non-verbal communication speaks volumes about you.
- Job candidates are evaluated based on non-verbal communication.
- Good communication skills are the foundation for successful relationships.
- Non-verbal communication is a powerful tool to connect and express what you mean.
- Non-verbal communication is eye contact, facial expression, gestures and posture when you communicate with others.
- Evaluate your non-verbal communication skills in your interactions with others.
- Negative body language can you hurt your career.
- Avoid unprofessional language which could put your career at risk.

CHAPTER SEVEN

WOMEN BODY LANGUAGE

Women
The Power of Silent Body Language

INTRODUCTION

What does your body language say to others about you?

Silent body language is an effective business tool for women to use in the workplace. Non-verbal communication adds confidence, power and authority to interactions with management and co-workers. Non-verbal signals are important and should be intentional. Listed are body language principles to enhance your communication at work.

Body Language: Ten Power and Authority Principles

Principle One: Head Tilt
- Limit how often you tilt your head.
- Project power and authority by holding your head straight up during interactions.

Principle Two: Physical Height and Space
- Stand tall with your shoulders back.
- Hold your head up high.
- Arrive early and claim your space at meetings and conferences by spreading your belongings out in your space.
- At meetings sit up front – the power seat is to the right of the speaker.

Principle Three: Gestures
- Use hand gestures to reinforce your verbal communication.
- Turn your hands palm down when you are confident in your position.

Principle Four: Speak Up
- Use a professional and respectful authoritative tone in your communication.

Principle Five: Smile
- Smiling is a powerful non-verbal communication signal.
- Smiling communicates friendliness and likeability.
- Avoid smiling when the communication is serious.

Principle Six: Nodding your Head
- Do not nod your head to much.

- Nodding your head can express agreement, encouragement and engagement – not power and authority.
- When you express your opinion – keep your head still it shows confidence, power and authority.

Principle Seven: Learn to Interrupt
- Be professional and respectful – learn to interrupt to make your point.

Principle Eight: Minimize your Movements
- Minimize your movement in situations where you need to maximize your authority.
- Minimize your hand gestures.
- A calm appearance gives you power and authority.

Principle Nine: Do Not Flirt
- Come across as a competent professional – do not engage in flirtatious behavior.

Principle Ten: Professional Handshake
- A smile and a professional handshake are business assets.
- Make a palm-to-palm handshake.
- Give direct eye contact when you shake hands.
- Shake the other person's hand firmly.
- When you speak: "It's good to meet you" or what is appropriate for the greeting.

Summary

Women: The Power of Silent Body Language

Key Points:
- A smile and a professional handshake are business assets.
- A smile communicates friendliness and likeability.
- Use your hands to reinforce verbal communication.
- When you express your opinion keep your hands still – it shows power and authority.
- Minimize your movements to show confidence, power and authority.
- Arrive early at meetings and conferences to claim your space.
- The Power Seat - At meetings and conferences sit up front to the right of the speaker.

CHAPTER EIGHT

LEADERSHIP

Leadership
Essential Leadership Skills in the New Workplace

INTRODUCTION

Do you want a good job? Do you have leadership skills?

It's estimated over thirty percent of companies are looking for leaders to move into executive positions. Are you friendly? Do you like people? Are you approachable? Leadership skills are essential to be on the fast track for a successful leader.

No matter where you are in your career – a student, college graduate or working professional it's never to early to develop leadership skills. Leadership skills enhance your self-esteem, improve work habits, train you how to delegate assignments, evaluate performance, resolve conflict, and manage customer service issues and other skills. Contemporary leadership skills provide new ways to lead in the new workplace. Listed are effective leadership rules.

Twelve New Rules of Leadership

Rule 1: Lead and Deliver on Commitments
- Make a commitment to complete all assignments.
- Work hard and discipline yourself to follow-up.

Rule 2: Lead and Master Communication Skills
- Understand communication is two-way.
- Use creativity to articulate ideas, strategies, techniques and visions.
- Listen with your eyes, ears, heart and mind.

Rule 3: Lead with Confidence
- Project confidence to gain the respect of others.
- Have confidence in yourself and abilities.

Rule 4: Lead and Be Courageous
- Have the courage to confront new situations.
- Be a risk taker.
- Speak up about important things.
- Speak up about expectations from those you lead.
- Face challenges and overcome obstacles to achieve company goals.

Rule 5: Lead and Share Enthusiasm
- Motivate your team to be top performers.
- Have high energy and the ability to energize your team.

Rule 6: Lead by Example
- Practice what you preach and lead by example.

Rule 7: Lead with Integrity
- Leaders have high ethics.
- Leaders are honest.
- Take responsibility for your actions.

- Take responsibility for the actions and results of your team performance.

Rule 8: Lead to Develop People
- Leaders have the ability to develop others.
- Leaders build a strong team.
- Leaders observe the behavior of others.
- Leaders learn the strengths and weaknesses of the team members.
- Leaders build relationships with the team and team members.

Rule 9: Lead and Set Priorities
- Leaders do the most important things first.
- Leaders put forth effort to do things right.

Rule 10: Lead and Take Personal Responsibility
- Leaders take responsibility when things go wrong.
- Leaders who take responsibility shows integrity, gain trust and respect of team members.

Rule 11: Lead to be Solution-Oriented
- Leaders focus on the solution not the problem.
- Leaders develop a plan and strategy to achieve objectives.
- Leaders set priorities to address the most important urgent things.

Rule 12: Lead and Share Successes
- Leaders share the successes with their team.
- Leaders show the results of their achievements.
- Leaders are only as good as the teams they develop.

Summary

Leadership

Key Points:
- Leaders are in demand by employers.
- Leaders master their communication skills.
- Leaders have self confidence.
- Leaders are courageous.
- Leaders act with integrity.
- Leaders develop people.
- Leaders take personal responsibility.
- Leaders are solution-oriented.

CHAPTER NINE

NEGOTIATION SKILLS

Effective Negotiation Skills Are Critical At Work

INTRODUCTION

What is Negotiation? The Definition

Negotiation is determining a solution which results in a win-win solution acceptable to both parties.

Do you know how to negotiate?

Negotiation skills are necessary for the workplace, salary negotiations and personal relationships. The most successful negotiators use the following skills to be effective.

Six Essential Skills of Negotiators

1. Plan Ahead
- Take time to analyze the situation.
- Think through your strategy.
- Make a list of your needs and wants.
- Make a list of the other person's need and wants.

2. Outcomes and Options
- Consider various outcomes and options.
- Do not insist on specific results.
- Have an open mind for best results.
- Consider multiple possibilities.
- Consider combinations of options.

3. Common Ground
- Look for common ground – not conflict.

4. Discuss Key Issues
- Discuss key issues based on priority.
- Identify top and less important issues.
- Agreement on important issues will make lesser issues easier to resolve.

5. Cooperation
- Avoid annoying behaviors such as being aggressive, intimidating, sarcasm, negative body language and others.
- Work hard at being open, responsible and friendly.

6. Avoid Attacks
- Avoid defend – attack strategies.
- Avoid language that is aggressive or defensive.

It takes practice to get what you want in negotiation. Negotiation skills will enable you to reach agreements for a win-win solution and maintain positive relationships. These negotiation skills will help you achieve your goals in the workplace or at home.

Negotiation: Six Tips to Enhance Your Negotiation Skills

Negotiation skills help you resolve conflicts. Do not attempt to use an aggressive approach to avoid damaging the relationship – however do not be passive which could be a disadvantage for you.

Six Tips to Enhance Your Negotiation Skills

Tip 1: Develop Relationships
- Developing relationships is a valuable negotiation tool.
- Value relationships you can leverage to your advantage.

Tip 2: When to Say NO
- Do not be afraid to say NO – to get what you want.
- Be willing to walk away if the negotiation process becomes aggressive.
- When you stand for something – you will gain respect.
- Stand your ground – be assertive and be determined to negotiate what you want.

Tip 3: Gather Information about Your Opponents
- Always gather important information about your opponents.
- Brainstorm how you will approach the negotiation process.

Tip 4: Make a List – What Do You Want? What Do You Have to Offer

- Make a detail list of what you want from the negotiations and what you have to offer.
- Identify what you bring to the bargaining table.
- Make a powerful presentation so it will be difficult for your opponent to say no.
- Make it easy for your opponent to say yes.

Tip 5: Control your Emotions

- Always maintain control of your emotions.
- Be calm and maintain your professionalism at all times.
- If you feel you need a time out to regroup – ask for it.

Tip 6: It's Not Personal

- Do not take negotiations personally if you do not get what you want.
- Focus on building long-term relationships with your opponent.
- Be willing to gain less to gain valuable business relationships.

Summary

Negotiation Skills

Key Points:

- Negotiation is determining a solution which results in a win-win solution that is acceptable to both parties.
- Plan ahead is one of the essential skills of negotiators.
- It takes practice to get what you want in negotiation.
- Developing relationships is a valuable negotiation tool.

- Do not be afraid to say no – to get what you want.
- Always gather important information about your opponents.
- Make a list of what you want and what you have to offer.

"A professional image helps you sell your message."
-PATRICIA DORCH

SALARY NEGOTIATION

The Power of Salary Negotiation

INTRODUCTION

Can you effectively negotiate your salary and benefits package?

Salary negotiation is an essential skill all professionals should possess. Many professionals are uncomfortable negotiating their salary and benefits package – as a result they often accept a salary lower than what whey are worth. Effective salary negotiation skills will ensure you will receive top salary and benefits for your work experience.

Visual Presentation and Perception Add Value

At your final interview you will probably meet with one or more multiple managers or a company executive. Create a perception of value in your appearance and use business tools that make you stand out and more valuable than your competition.

Dress for Success – Professional Appearance
- Dress in a quality business suit for your final interview and possible job offer – show your value – perception is everything.

Resume Portfolio
- Put your resume, references and other essential documents in a portfolio with your personal business card on the outside of the portfolio.

Writing Tablet and Pen
- Pull out your leather writing tablet and quality ink pen even though you do not need to write anything down – perception of your business tools add value to your offer.

Final Interview Thank-you

After your final interview send an *email* thank you letter immediately to your contacts. Call – *do not* email the contacts that previously interviewed you – timing is everything. Thank your interviewers for their support during the interview process and inform them when the final decision will be made.

Use this strategy to effectively position yourself as a top candidate – raise the bar and expectations for other candidates. When the interviewers make their hiring decision, you will have made a lasting impression. They will remember you – your skills and the professionalism you demonstrated during the interview process. Listed are salary negotiation secrets you should use prior to being offered the job.

Eight Secrets of Salary Negotiation

Secret One: Research – Know What You Are Worth
- Do your research to determine what the current salary range is for someone with your knowledge, skills, abilities and education in your current market.

Secret Two: Salary Range

- Never state the salary you want without knowing the salary range. The unspoken rule is the first person who states an amount loses their negotiation power.
- *Always* ask what the salary range is *before* you state a desired amount.

Listed is an example to illustrate what can happen when you request a salary without the knowledge of a salary range.

CANDIDATE 1

Hiring Manager:
What salary are you expecting for this position?
Candidate:
I would like a base salary of $55,000 per year – plus benefits.
Hiring Manager:
Great! – I accept your salary request and will prepare the Letter of Offer for you.

CANDIDATE 2

Hiring Manager:
What are your salary expectations for this position?
Candidate:
Could you share with me what the salary range is for this position?
Hiring Manager:
Yes, the salary range is between $55,000 - $65,000 per year – plus benefits.
Candidate:
Based on the value of my experience you discussed during my interviews – I believe $65,000 is appropriate.

Although your salary might not start at $65,000 per year – starting at the top of the range increases your chances of negotiating a desired income based on your ability to perform the job and sell your skills. When you state a lower salary figure without knowledge of the range it's difficult to increase what you initially stated you wanted. You have also communicated your lack of negotiation skills by stating a figure before you know the details of the offer.

Candidate 1 - possibly has lost $10,000 per year – if you were employed for a minimum of two years a salary loss of $20,000.00. It will be difficult to make up what you have lost. Your goal is to get paid what you are worth – the hiring manager's goal is to hire the most qualified candidate at the least amount of cost to their organization.

Secret Three: Start at the Top of the Salary Range
- Once you know the salary range start at the top. When you start at the top of the salary range it leaves room to negotiate with your employer based on your experience. You can not negotiate up once you state a lower amount.

Secret Four: Always Negotiate the Salary Offer
- If you are offered a salary, *always* ask for more than you are offered – you will be *respected* for it.
- Employers expect to negotiate when they see you are comfortable asking for more money.
- Be prepared to *sell* your skills and explain why you should be paid more than the first offer presented to you.

Secret Five: Take Risks in Negotiation
- Be prepared to confidently provide examples of why you add value to the position and want more money.

Secret Six: Know When To Stop Negotiations

- Do not engage in a salary war at the risk of losing the support of the employer or the job offer.

Secret Seven: New Hire Bonus

- Once your salary is negotiated ask if there is a *"new hire"* bonus – a secret in the industry that no one will tell you. Not all companies have a new hire bonus – however you will not know unless you ask.

Secret Eight: Get It in Writing

- Always get the job offer – salary, bonus and commission program, benefits and start date in writing before you give notice at your current employer if you are working.

Summary

Salary Negotiation

Key Points:

- Every professional should be capable of negotiating their salary and benefits.
- Each step you make leading to your job offer should be strategically planned.
- Your salary expectations should be negotiable based on your skill set and the current job market.
- The goal of salary negotiations is a win-win for both parties - give and take for a successful outcome.
- Visual presentation and perception add value to salary negotiation.
- There are eight salary negotiation secrets you should use prior to your job offer.

- Starting at the top of the salary range is a negotiation secret.
- Always negotiate your salary and not feel obligated to accept the first offer.

CHAPTER TEN

PROBLEM SOLVING

Problem Solving
How to Use the PAR Formula to Solve Problems

INTRODUCTION

Are you a problem solver? Do you know how to analyze a problem and solve it?

P roblem-solving is a required and important skill every professional needs to get hired, promoted and achieve organizational goals.

What is a problem? The Definition

A problem is something that is not planned and deviation from the norm.

How quickly can you solve a problem?

Use a road map to define the problem, brainstorm alternatives, and implement an action plan to get desired results. Use the

PAR Formula strategies as a guide to problem solve.

THE PAR FORMULA (PROBLEM, ACTION AND RESULTS)

Three Strategies to Problem Solve

Strategy One: Problem – Identify and Clearly Define the Problem

1. **Problem.** What is the problem?
2. **Discovery.** Did you identify the problem or was it brought to your attention.
3. **Who.** Who does this problem affect?
4. **What.** What is the effect of the problem?
5. **When.** When did this problem occur?
6. **Where.** Where did this problem start?
7. **Why?** Why did this problem occur?
8. **How?** How often does this problem happen?

Strategy Two: Action – Develop an Action Plan

1. **Action Steps.** What action steps will you use to solve the problems?
2. **Options.** What are your options?
3. **Resources.** What do you need to solve the problem?
4. **Independent or Team.** Can you solve the problem alone or will you need assistance?
5. **Costs.** Are there costs associated with solving the problem?
6. **Barriers.** Is there time or other barriers associated with solving the problem?
7. **Approval.** Can you solve the problem without management approval? Are you a risk taker?
8. **Strategy.** If your plan requires management approval – how will you present and support your action plan?

9. **Target Date.** Can I implement my plan immediately or will I need to set a target date?
10. **Resolved.** Who will I need to inform the problem is solved?

Strategy Three: Results – How to Evaluate Results
1. **Action Plan.** What are the results of the action plan?
2. **Conclusion.** How well did you solve the problem?
3. **Options.** What would you do differently? Why?
4. **Root Causes.** What did you learn that is beneficial to solve future problem?

Problem solving skills will enable you to increase your career options, accountability, responsibility, visibility and value to an employer.

Summary

Problem Solving

Key Points:
- Problem-solving is a required and important skill for every professional.
- Problem-solving is something that is not planned and a deviation from the norm.
- The PAR Formula is used to strategically solve problems.
- There are three strategies to problem solve – **P**roblem, **A**ction and **R**esults.
- Problem-solving skills increase your career opportunities.

CHAPTER ELEVEN

PROFESSIONALISM

What is Professionalism?
Professionalism in the Workplace

INTRODUCTION

What is Professionalism? Do you have the professionalism skills you need to be successful?

Professionalism is associated with the attitude, behavior and perception of an employee in the workplace.

Are You A Professional?

Professionalism in the workplace is essential to every organization in the 21st Century. Every employer has rules and standards how employees are expected to act regardless of race, religion, sex, sexual orientation and diverse differences.

Everything you do whether you are on or off the clock matters to your employer. Your behavior is a reflection of your employer – never underestimate the power and action of your employer when your behavior is inappropriate.

Could Your Career Be At Risk?

Always conduct yourself in a professional manner – manage difficult situations with tact and class. Do not put your career at risk in public and private settings – someone is always watching you and possibly taking a picture of you with an electronic device.

Do You Adhere To Company Rules?

Employees should maintain a level of professionalism in the workplace and adhere to employer's written and unwritten rules, expectations and code of ethics guidelines for – adherence to confidentiality agreements, data privacy, conflict resolution, business accountability and other policies and procedures.

Think Before You Hit "SEND"

Think *before* you hit the send button when using electronic devices at work and social media. You are judged by what you say, how you say it and your circle of influence.

Not all pictures should be shared on social media. Be mindful of images you share with family and friends that may appear on social media without your knowledge. These images will follow you throughout your career and "silently" prevent you from getting hired or promoted – in fact they might get you terminated.

Sharing Too Much Information (TMI)

Are you sharing too much information about your personal or professional life on social media? Employers frequently check social media websites to find out information about their employees. When your behavior is not consistent with the company's expectations you are a "career risk" for your employer and could possibly lose your job or not get hired.

How Do You Look?

The corporate culture has become relaxed over the years with business casual attire which has increased unprofessional behavior and relaxed standards. How you look, act and communicate determines whether you are a professional. Listed are professional characteristics and unprofessional traits you should avoid in your career.

Seventeen Top Characteristics of a Professional Employee

1. **Integrity.** Make the correct choice when faced with the right or wrong decision.
2. **Professional Appearance.** Wear professional attire and accessories minus visible tattoos and non-religious piercings.
3. **Communication Skills.** Excellent oral and written communication skills.
4. **Attitude and Behavior.** Maintains a positive attitude and professional behavior.
5. **Active Listening.** Listen to what is said and not said.
6. **Work Ethic.** Demonstrates a good work ethic and completes assignments on time.
7. **Self Confidence.** Has a can do attitude.

8. **Self Control.** Knows how to control emotions.
9. **Self Awareness.** Understand your personal style and adapts to others.
10. **Interpersonal Skills.** Positive and engaging interpersonal skills.
11. **Manners.** Shows manners and courtesy to others.
12. **Respect.** Respects others and their time.
13. **Etiquette.** Has business and dining etiquette - good manners and polish.
14. **Accountability.** Accepts accountability and responsibility for business decisions.
15. **Independent.** Flexible and adaptable to work situation.
16. **Purpose.** Has a sense of direction and purpose.
17. **Entitlement.** Has no attitude of career entitlement.

Thirteen "Red Flag" Traits of an Unprofessional Employee

Are You Unprofessional?

Employees serious about their careers should create an action plan to improve their unprofessional traits. To have a successful career and achieve your professional goals address the traits that can prevent you from being considered for employment and promotions.

Thirteen "Red Flag" Traits of an Unprofessional Employee

Could this be you?
1. **Integrity.** Lacks integrity.
2. **Professional Appearance.** Unprofessional attire, visible tattoos and non-religious piercing.
3. **Communication Skills.** Lacks good oral and written communication skills.

4. **Attitude.** Poor attitude – negative behavior.
5. **Listening Skills.** Does not listen when others speak.
6. **Work Ethic.** Poor work ethic – does not take work seriously or complete tasks on time.
7. **Self Confidence.** Lacks self confidence – frequently needs assurance to accomplish goals.
8. **Self Control.** Unable to control emotions.
9. **Self Awareness.** Lacks self awareness – does not have the communication skills to adapt to others.
10. **People Skills.** Lacks positive interaction skills.
11. **Courtesy.** Does not show courtesy to others.
12. **Disrespectful.** Disrespectful to others.
13. **Etiquette.** Lacks business and dining etiquette, manners and polish.

Professionals are valued employees who positively impact the company culture – their experience makes then indispensable. They focus on profitable results, are productive, results oriented and deliver exceptional quality for their employer. Professionalism is important at the individual and corporate levels in the workplace.

Summary

Professionalism
- Professionalism characteristics will set you apart from other employees.
- Career success begins with professionalism.
- Professionalism is valued in the job market.
- Professionals know how to deliver their best work.
- Professionals are accountable, responsible and productive.

- There are "red flag" traits of an unprofessional employee which can prevent you from being hired and promoted.
- Professionalism is important at the individual and corporate levels in the workplace.

For more information about professionalism I recommend my book: ***Professionalism: New Rules for Workplace Career Success.***

Visit: www.whatisprofessionalism.com

CHAPTER TWELVE

PERSONAL ACCOUNTABILITY

**Personal Accountability
How to Be Accountable**

INTRODUCTION

Are you accountable and responsible for your work?

Personal accountability is an important business skill. Employees are expected to take ownership of assigned tasks and results without making excuses for outcomes that are not positive. Your accountability and responsibility impacts the performance, productivity and profitability of the organization. Listed are ways personal accountability affects your performance in the workplace.

Twenty Personal Accountability Principles

Principle 1: Accountability
- Accountability keeps you grounded and reminds you of your responsibility.

Principle 2: Admit Mistakes

- Admit your mistakes and be willing to do whatever it takes to correct the situation.

Principle 3: Choose Your Battles

- Use wisdom, knowledge and understanding in making a decision which issues are worth the effort and those that are not.
- Not every issue is important enough to be fought.

Principle 4: Commitments

- Commitments are expected to be kept.

Principle 5: Conflict

- Conflict is inevitable the way you respond is your choice.

Principle 6: Correction

- Accept correction and do not be rebellious.

Principle 7: Go The Extra Mile

- When asked by management to work overtime – go the extra mile to get the job done.

Principle 8: Gossip

- Spreading gossip about others can hurt their reputation and damage relationships.

Principle 9: Integrity

- Make the right choice when faced with a dishonest act.

Principle 10: Listen

- Listen and be open to advice from management and co-workers.

Principle 11: Manage Your Words
- Speak wisely and positively about co-workers and management.

Principle 12: Recognize Your Personal Power
- Use personal power to manage your career and achieve the skills required to be successful.
- No one can give you personal power or take it away from you.

Principle 13: Reputation
- A good reputation is more valuable than money and power.

Principle 14: Respect
- Set your standard by respecting others whether they respect you or not.

Principle 15: Self-Control
- Reserve your thoughts and emotions in certain situations.
- Take time to process information before you react to make a wise decision.

Principle 16: Self Development
- Enhance your skill set by taking professional development courses.

Principle 17: Take Ownership
- Personal accountability and responsibility prevents the "blame game" when tasks and projects are assigned to you.

Principle 18: Teamwork
- Work with your team and learn from differences, shared goals, benefits and celebrate the rewards.

Principle 19: Toot Your Horn
- In a professional manner and at the right time let management know of your talents, achievements and how they contributed to the success of your department.

Principle 20: Visibility
- Arrive early to work and stay late when possible.

Meetings
- Be visible at meetings - sit up front to the right of the speaker.
- Speak up and make a contribution and volunteer to pass out handouts.

Volunteer
- Volunteer for a new project or help a co-worker complete a project.

Summary

Personal Accountability

Key Points:
- Personal accountability is an important business skill.
- Accountability and responsibility impacts the performance, productivity and profitability of the organization.

- Every employee is accountable and responsible for performing their jobs at the highest standards for their organizations.
- Personal accountability takes courage, integrity, self confidence and self examination.
- Accountability promotes your professionalism, distinguishes you from others and essential to your success.

ACCOUNTABILITY

Accountability impacts performance, productivity and profitability of the organization.

Conflict is inevitable the way you respond is your choice.

Commitments are expected to be met on time.

Oral and written communication skills are essential to accomplish workplace goals.

Understand what is expected of you.

No one can give your personal power or take it away from you.

Take ownership when tasks and projects are assigned to you.

Admit your mistakes and be willing to do whatever it takes to correct the situation.

Be willing to take risks for career advancement.

Integrity requires you to make the right choice when faced with a dishonest act.

Listen and be open to advice from management and co-workers.

Identify skills you need to learn or enhance.

Take the initiative to be open to new challenges.

You will be successful by being accountable and responsible for your decisions.

CHAPTER THIRTEEN

TEAMWORK ACCOUNTABILITY

Teamwork Accountability Qualities

INTRODUCTION

Are you accountable to your team members? How do your team members feel about you?

No matter what your position is in the workplace you are accountable to others for your actions. Teamwork is the interest and ability to work together for common goals. Team members are accountable to each other in easy and difficult times.

Team members should embrace five core qualities to be accountable – character, competence, commitment, consistency and cohesion. Listed are accountability qualities to build a team.

Five Teamwork Accountability Qualities

1. Character - Trust
- Build a team culture of individuals you can trust.
- Share successes.
- All accomplishments are done and celebrated together.
- No one fails alone.
- Do not keep secrets.
- All information is shared with team members.
- Depend on each other for facts and truth.
- Do not panic in tough times.
- Always keep your word.
- Say what you mean and mean what you say.
- Develop team member's abilities to be successful.
- Set high expectations and standards.
- Spend quality time together.
- Care about each other.
- Take pride in what you do.
- Losing is not an option.

2. Competence
- Competence and character matter.

3. Commitment
- Real team work requires commitment to achieve goals.
- Be confident you can count on your team members.
- Team members have a whatever it takes attitude.
- Team members are self motivated, self confident and productive.
- Team members have enthusiasm and passion.

4. Consistency
- The ability for team members to consistently function at a higher level.

- Team members need to stick together no matter how difficult the situation.

5. Cohesion
- Team members must be accountable to each other.

How Do You Perform As A Team Leader?

- Do you have good *character*? Can others *trust* you?
- Do you perform your work with *competence*?
- Do you make a *commitment* to team success?
- Are you *consistent*? Can others depend on you?
- Can you bring a team together – *cohesion*?

Summary

Teamwork Accountability

Key Points:
- No matter what your position in the workplace you are accountable to others for your actions.
- Team members are accountable to each others in easy and difficult times.
- There are five core qualities of team accountability.
- Character is a core quality of accountability.
- Real team work requires commitment to achieve goals.

WHAT ARE

SOFT**SKILLS**?

TOP SECONDARY SOFT SKILLS

CHAPTER FOURTEEN

DECISION MAKING

Effective Decision Making

INTRODUCTION

Are you capable of making decisions in the workplace?

Making good accountable decisions is an important skill required in the workplace. Everyday we are faced with making decision. In college-you make a decision to attend class, study for an exam, work on an assignment and achieve the requirements to graduate. In the workplace you are expected to make decisions to attend meetings, meet with clients and vendors, supervise your team and manage important day to day responsibilities.

Are you productive?

Decisions you make in the workplace contribute to the productivity of your department and organization. There is a direct relationship between decision making and productivity. Decision making can be simple or involve more complex issues. Listed are types of decision making for complex issues.

Five Types of Decision Making for Complex Issues:

Type 1: Alternatives – Options and Consequences
Type 2: Complexity – Interrelated Factors
Type 3: High Risk – Consequences of Decisions
Type 4: Interpersonal Issues – How People May React
Type 5: Uncertainty – Unknown Facts

The Decision Making Process Critical Steps of Making a Good Decision

A decision making process helps you use essential tools to approach your decision and make the right choice. Making good decisions requires a decision making process that may lead to consistent quality results. Listed are critical steps to make decisions.

Six Critical Steps of Decision Making

Step 1: What is the Purpose?
- Define specifically what you want to accomplish.

Step 2: Determine the Process
- How will the decision be made?
- Will the decision be made by an individual or team?
- Will the decision have fallback options or alternatives?

Step 3: Consult with the Right People
- Consult with key stakeholders before a decision is determined.
- Do not create an atmosphere where team members are competing for the best decision.

Step 4: Encourage Opinions
- Encourage all team members to be heard.

Step 5: Ask the Right Questions
- Confirm the right issue or purpose – to ask the right questions to get the best outcome.

Step 6: Be Creative
- Be creative in your thought process.
- Use creativity to explore alternatives.
- Use creativity to generate new ideas.

Leadership Decision Making: Six Steps of Leadership Decision Making

Are you confident about the decisions you make?

Leaders are faced with making many decisions in the workplace. The perception of employees and outcome play an important role in these decisions. No matter what the outcome – the perception and the reputation of a leader is at stake. Listed are steps for leaders to make decisions.

Six Steps of Leadership Decision Making

Step One: Make Decisions Alone
- Leader makes decisions where no input is required or there is no time to seek input from others.

Step Two: Input from Team Members
- Leader gathers input from team to gain feedback about the issue to make a decision.

Step Three: Gathers Input from Internal Associates
- Leader meets with internal associates to discuss ideas, and gathers information to make a decision.

Step Four: Agreement Building
- Leader seeks thoughts and opinions until consensus is reached and everyone is confident with the decision.

Step Five: Delegates the Decision
- Leader delegates the decision to the team what criteria need to be met before the decision is final.
- Leader informs the team of possible options.

Step Six: Fallback Option
- When the designated team does not have consensus for a decision the leader will use the fallback option to make the decision.

Summary

Effective Decision Making

Key Points:
- Decision making is an important skill in the workplace.
- There are five types of decision making for complex issues.
- There are six critical steps of decision making.
- No matter what the outcome – the perception and the reputation of a leader is at stake.
- The fallback option allows the leader to make the decision when the team does not have a consensus.

CHAPTER FIFTEEN

ENTHUSIASM

Enthusiasm
The Key to a Successful Future

INTRODUCTION

Are you enthusiastic? Do you show enthusiasm during the interview process?

Enthusiasm is the energy you bring to the position which is essential to career success. When you interview for a new job or promotion show enthusiasm and you will "stand out" from other candidates. Prepare quality interview questions that will demonstrate you interest, desire and excitement about the company. Once hired continue to demonstrate enthusiasm in electronic, written and oral communication with management, co-workers, customers and clients.

If you are required to bring ideas to meetings and conferences, take time to put them in *writing* and email them to the host of the meeting and copy in your manager prior to the meeting day. This will allow time for the host to review your ideas and possibly discuss them during the event. Always bring a few copies of your written ideas to the meeting. If you are a "visual" person bring a mock-up of a product idea to the meeting or event - it does not need to be perfect only to convey your idea.

Enthusiasm is the secret strategy which allows you to "stand out" from your peers; it shows the time and effort you took to make a contribution – which will not go unnoticed by management and executives. If management likes your idea and it's implemented – it shows your interest, ownership of the project and commitment to the company. Enthusiasm can positively impact your performance review and position you for promotional opportunities.

How Do You Develop Enthusiasm? Six Ways to Develop Enthusiasm

1. Personal Quote
- Develop a personal quote that excites you.
- Repeat your quote out loud throughout the day.
- At the end of the day identify good things that happened to you.

2. Great Day Expectancy
- Project a great day expectant attitude everyday.

3. Control Your Mind
- Realize you control your mind emotions and thoughts.
- You become what you think.

4. Quality of Thoughts
- Let go of thoughts that do not contribute to your well being.

5. Professional Appearance
- Your professional appearance communicates who you are, where you are mentally and where you are going in your career.

6. Leverage the Power of Enthusiasm
- Successful people use enthusiasm to "stand out' and get hired.
- Successful people use enthusiasm to get them through challenging times.
- Successful people use enthusiasm to learn from everyone.

What Are the Benefits of Enthusiasm?

Ten Benefits of Enthusiasm

1. Listen
- Enthusiasm inspires your audience to listen to your message.

2. Influence
- Enthusiasm is an essential ingredient used to influence others.

3. Stand Out
- Enthusiasm helps you to "stand out" and be more visible at work.

4. Ideas
- Enthusiasm is used to promote your ideas and contribute to the success of the organization.

5. Inspire

- Enthusiasm helps you to engage, motivate and inspire others.

6. Confidence

- Enthusiasm shows you have confidence in what you are communicating to others.

7. Interest

- Enthusiasm captures the interest in people who you are communicating to.

8. Career

- Enthusiasm is used to build a successful career.

9. Impress

- Enthusiasm can be used to impress management and others with your abilities.

10. Focus

- Enthusiasm helps you stay focused to get things done.

Summary

Enthusiasm

Key Points:

- Enthusiasm is the energy you bring to the career opportunity or event.
- Use enthusiasm in electronic, written and oral communication.

- Show enthusiasm in meetings, conferences and events by documenting your ideas.
- Enthusiasm is used to promote your ideas and contribute to the success of the organization.
- Enthusiasm does not go unnoticed by management and executives.
- A professional appearance communicates how enthusiastic you are about what you do.
- Enthusiasm will make you "stand out" from your peers.
- Enthusiasm shows you have confidence in what you are communicating to others.
- Enthusiasm will make you more visible in the organization.

CHAPTER SIXTEEN

INTEGRITY

Integrity for Today's Workplace

INTRODUCTION

Do you act with integrity in the workplace?

Integrity is an important characteristic of every professional and your secret to success. A person of integrity is expected to make the right choice when faced with a right or wrong decision. You will be more successful at work and earn the respect of your employer by maintaining integrity. Integrity builds a positive reputation and long-term relationships for you and your employer. Professionals who have integrity possess the following characteristics for success.

Eleven Integrity Characteristics for Success

1. **Accountable.** Accountable and responsible.
2. **Authentic.** Authentic and straightforward.

3. **Behavior.** Behavior is consistent with values.
4. **Character.** Strength of character.
5. **Commitment.** Delivers on commitments.
6. **Differences.** Understands and respects differences.
7. **Goodness.** Believes in the goodness of others.
8. **Maturity.** Maturity and wisdom.
9. **Respect.** Respects authority and others.
10. **Self Awareness.** Understand your personal style and learn how to adapt to others.
11. **Values.** Have clear values when making decisions and knows the difference between right and wrong.

Integrity is a reflection of a person's character and should never be compromised. Listed are ways to apply integrity principles at work.

Ten Integrity Success Principles

Success Principle One: Employer's Time
- Show up to work on time.
- Do not leave work before your designated time.
- Return from breaks and lunch on time.
- If you are late and do not use a time clock – inform your supervisor of your arrival time and apologize for being late.

Success Principle Two: Do Not Bad Mouth Your Employer

- With other colleagues.
- During and after business hours.
- In public places – such as industry organizations, meetings, restaurants, seminars and workshops.
- On social networking websites.

- On teleconferences – you never know who is on the line without your knowledge.
- In the restroom.

Success Principle Three: Maintain Confidentiality
- Abide by your company's policies and procedures you agreed to in your employment agreement.

Success Principle Four: Accountable
- Get your work done on time and keep commitments.

Success Principle Five: Company Breaks
- Take only the designated time allowed for breaks and lunch breaks.
- Do not take more breaks than has been authorized by your employer.

Success Principle Six: Mistakes
- If you make a mistake correct it and inform those individuals who needs to be aware of the situation.
- Making mistakes is a learning process – everyone makes them.
- *Always* apologize for your mistake.

Success Principle Seven: You Are Judged by the Company You Keep
- Do not associate with individuals who have a reputation for gossiping or who do not take their work seriously.
- Socializing with the wrong employees will give the perception you act and behave as they do and will limit your career success.
- Know your Circle of Influence.

Success Principle Eight: Tell the Truth
- Always tell the truth.

Success Principle Nine: Be Reliable
- Be reliable and keep all commitments.
- If you can not keep a commitment notify the proper people in a timely manner.

Success Principle Ten: Social Networking
- Posting information on social networking sites without company permission regarding your employer, management or colleagues can be a career-limiting move (CLM). Refer to your company's employee handbook for clarification.

Summary

Integrity

Key Points:
- Integrity is ranked as one of the most important characteristics of an employee.
- Professionals who have integrity possess essential success characteristics.
- Integrity begins before a person is faced with a right or wrong decision.
- Without integrity individuals are not trustworthy.
- Integrity builds a positive reputation with your employer, co-workers and associates.
- Integrity is a reflection of a person's character and should never be compromised.

CHAPTER SEVENTEEN

LISTENING

The Power of Listening

INTRODUCTION

Are you a good listener? Do you actively listen to others when they speak?

One of the single most important things you can do to get hired, promoted and excel in the workplace is the power of listening. During the interview process interviewers assess how well you listen to questions based on your responses.

Listening to others will open your eyes, ears, heart and mind and see things from the speaker's perspective. A good listener is aware of the looks, attitudes and body language of others.

Listening will enable you to be productive, influence others, avoid conflicts and reduce misunderstanding. Listening to what is said – is as important as what is *not* said. Listed are reasons why listening is important.

Five Reasons Listening is Important

Reason 1: To gain valuable information.
Reason 2: Respect the person who is speaking.
Reason 3: Get along with others.
Reason 4: Gain insight about the other person's thoughts and behavior.
Reason 5: Makes it easier to deal with others and their emotions.

Active Listening: Fifteen New Techniques for Active Listening

Are you an active listener? Do your listening skills need improvement?

Active listening is twice as hard as talking – it takes practice to acquire good listening skills. Information is sent by a speaker and received by an active listener. By moving your face and keeping your eyes on the speaker you can easily adapt good listening skills.

An open mind will let you concentrate on the message and receive information. Listed are techniques to strengthen your listening skills.

Fifteen New Techniques for Active Listening

Technique One: Look
- Look at the person who is speaking.

Technique Two: Eye Contact
- Establish eye contact with the speaker.

Technique Three: Body Language
- Good listeners lead with their facial expressions and body language.

Technique Four: Concentrate
- Concentrate on the message.

Technique Five: Distractions
- Eliminate external distractions.

Technique Six: Write
- Write down questions you may need to ask.

Technique Seven: Evaluate
- Evaluate the message delivered.

Technique Eight: Conclusions
- Do not jump to conclusions.

Technique Nine: Listen
- Do not stop listening.

Technique Ten: Verbal and Non-Verbal Cues
- Be alert to verbal and non-verbal cues by the speaker.

Technique Eleven: Pay Attention
- Give the speaker your undivided attention.
- Maintain eye contact with the speaker.
- Watch the speaker's body language.

Technique Twelve: Involvement
- Show your involvement – listen with your body language.
- An appropriate nod, smile or short comment will let the speaker know you are engaged in the conversation.

Technique Thirteen: Feedback
- Ask questions to clarify your understanding.

Technique Fourteen: Respond
- Active listening helps you gain information so you can respond appropriately.
- Active listening shows respect and understanding to the speaker.

Technique Fifteen: Concentration
- Active listening requires you concentrate and focus on what is said.

Active listeners use listening techniques to gain insight and help resolve conflict.

Active Listeners:
1. **Probe** – Ask questions for clarification.
2. **Information** – Ask for detailed information to increase understanding.
3. **Interest** – Nod their head to show interest and agreement or understanding.

Active listening is essential to gain confidence, support and trust others. It demonstrates a desire to understand the speaker which requires concentration, discipline and interest.

Active Listener: Seventeen Team Member Strategies for Active Listening

The ability to actively listen is essential to the performance of team members and good communication. Listed are team member strategies for active listening.

Strategy One: Active Listener Requires Team Members to:
- Actively listen before you speak to encourage dialogue which can bring about positive results.
- Understand and be open to new ideas and viewpoints from other team members.
- Be open to criticism without becoming defensive.

Strategy Two: Active Participant
- Successful team members are active participants.
- Prepare to listen and actively participate in discussions.
- Engage the team to achieve goals.
- Take the initiative to motivate others to make things happen.
- Volunteer for assignments.
- Can do attitude – ask yourself what I can do to make the team successful.

Strategy Three: Adaptable
- Adapt to changing situations.
- Maintain your composure.
- Be flexible in considering and implementing new viewpoints.

Strategy Four: Commitment
- Cares about the success of the team.
- Shows a commitment to the team.
- Show up when they are required to attend a meeting.

Strategy Five: Communicates
- Clearly express their ideas, and thoughts to others.
- Respect other team players.
- Knows how and when to make a point in a confident, positive and respectful manner.

Strategy Six: Competent
- Have adequate skills to perform your job.
- Focus on the goal.
- Identify the facts, details and process to implement the plan.

Strategy Seven: Cooperation
- Works with others to accomplish goals.
- Brainstorms together to solve problems.
- Responds to requests for help with a positive attitude.

Strategy Eight: Disciplined

When you enjoy your work you tend to be more disciplined. Team members who are disciplined are those employees who:

- Think about the right things to do.
- Control your emotions.
- Manage their actions for the benefit of the team.

Strategy Nine: Enthusiastic
- Your enthusiasm is the source of energy you bring to your team.

Each Team member should:
- Be responsible for your own enthusiasm.
- Be positive.
- Believe in what you are doing to accomplish the goals of the team.
- Surround yourself with enthusiastic people.
- Strive for excellence.

Strategy Ten: Inspire
- Inspire others.

Strategy Eleven: Mission Driven
- Focus on the goals of the team.
- Let those in charge lead.
- Work for team accomplishments not individual achievement.
- Work WE not ME.
- Make a positive contribution to the team.

Strategy Twelve: Prepared
- Being prepared is the difference between successfully achieving goals and losing an important opportunity.
- Have a positive attitude.
- Take action.
- Assess the situation.
- Think about a strategy.
- Learn from mistakes.

Strategy Thirteen: Problem Solver
- Identifies and address problems and solutions.
- Do not blame others.

Strategy Fourteen: Relationships – Team Relationships

Team members are those who:
- Get along with others.
- Share experiences.
- Trust each other.
- Respect others and their differences.
- Share mutual enjoyment.
- Make others feel unique.
- Are good listeners.
- Ask the right questions.

Strategy Fifteen: Reliable
- Gets work done.
- Meets all commitments.
- Follows through on assignments.
- Consistent.
- Delivers good performance all the time.

Strategy Sixteen: Respectful
- Consistently treats others with courtesy and respect.
- Seeks to understand and learn from others.
- Have a sense of humor.
- Have fun – but not at the expense of others.
- Deal with other people in a professional manner.
- Contribute to the success of the team without drawing attention to them.
- Winning in a respectful manner.

Strategy Seventeen: Shares
- Information
- Knowledge
- Experience
- Keep other team members informed
- Takes the initiative to offer help
- Works with others to solve problems

Strategic Listening: Four Levels of Strategic Listening

How well do you listen to others?

One of the reasons why people do not understand one another is they do not listen, become distracted or do not understand what is being communicated.

Strategic listening allows you to hear information, understand what the message means connect with others and identify the purpose of the message. Listed are strategies to enhance your listening skills in business.

Four Levels of Strategic Listening

Level One: Information
- People want to communicate information to others.
- Listen for specific details.
- Ask – Who? What? When? Where? Why? And How?

Level Two: Understanding
- Listen to understand.
- Listen for the objective.
- Confirm your understanding.

Level Three: Connect with Others
- Connect with others on an emotional level.
- Listen; observe body language and vocal tone.
- Make others feel connected.

Level Four: Purpose
- Identify wants and needs.
- Identify the goal.
- Ask about expected outcomes.

Summary

The Power of Listening

Key Points:

- Listening skills are important to get hired, promoted and vital to your career success.
- A good listener is alert to the body language of others.
- Listening will enable you to be productive.
- Active listening takes practice to acquire good listening skills.
- Active listening is essential to gain confidence, support and trust of others.
- Listening will inspire you.
- Listening changes everything.
- There are four levels of strategic listening – information, understanding, connects with others and purpose.
- Never stop listening with your eyes, ears, heart and mind.
- Active listeners ask questions, gather detailed information and show interest.

CHAPTER EIGHTEEN

PEOPLE SKILLS

**Build Your People Skills:
How to Succeed At Work**

INTRODUCTION

Do you have people skills? Are you comfortable interacting with people you don't know as well as people you know?

People skills are required everyday to interact with others at college, work and in our personal lives. Interactions at work should be conducted in a professional manner. Everything you do at work or do not do is analyzed and scrutinized by management and your peers. To boost your people skills learn new strategies to build rapport, be confident, and show appreciation and other essential people skills. Listed are people skill strategies to help you be successful.

Twenty One Strategies to Improve People Skills

Strategy One: Above and Beyond
- Add value to your work by going above and beyond what is expected of you.

Strategy Two: Attitude
- Have a positive attitude about everything – even though it may be challenging.

Strategy Three: Actively Listen
- Actively listen when others speak.
- Process information before you speak.
- Confirm your understanding of what was said.

Strategy Four: Appreciation
- Show appreciation when others help you or give you advice.

Strategy Five: Approachable
- Be friendly and approachable by others.

Strategy Six: Complain
- Do not complain about your work.
- Do not complain about management or your peers.

Strategy Seven: Compliment Others
- Compliment others for their ideas, advice and support.

Strategy Eight: Confident
- Show confidence when you interact with others.
- Be confident in your ideas, actions and decisions around others.

Strategy Nine: Connect with Others
- Connect with management and co-workers.

Strategy Ten: Courteous
- Be courteous to everyone.

Strategy Eleven: Gossip
- Do not gossip or spread rumors.
- Gossiping hurts others and tarnishes reputations.

Strategy Twelve: Happy Hour
- Avoid "hot button" topics such as sex, religion, politics, money and personal health issues.
- Talk about positive current events, books, movies, cultural events, the arts, world events and others.

Strategy Thirteen: Observant
- Be observant about what you see and hear.

Strategy Fourteen: Office
- Keep non business conversations short.
- Be observant and aware of others reactions when you visit their cubicles or office space unannounced. Always ask "Is this a good time?" – do not be offended if you are asked to come back or schedule a specific time to talk.

Strategy Fifteen: Patient
- Be patient with others and yourself when you learn new information.

Strategy Sixteen: Remember People's Name and Pronunciation
- Remember people's names and how to pronounce them.

- Using a person's name when you speak with them in person or on the phone is more personal.

Strategy Seventeen: Self Assess your People Skills
- Evaluate your own people skills.
- Do you have strong or weak people skills?
- Use people skills to improve your interactions.

Strategy Eighteen: Smile
- Smile and be friendly to management, co-workers and customers.

Strategy Nineteen: Supportive
- Be supportive of others ideas.

Strategy Twenty: Treat Others with Respect
- Treat everyone with respect.

Strategy Twenty One: Thank you – Say Thank you
- Write an email thank you, or give a thank you card to show appreciation for what someone has done for you.

Summary

People Skills

Key Points:
- People skills are used everyday to interact with people at college, work and in your personal lives.
- Everything you do or do not do at work is being analyzed and scrutinized by management and your peers.

- There are twenty one strategies to improve your people skills.
- Interactions at work should always be conducted in a professional manner.
- Show your appreciation when others assist you by saying "thank you."

CHAPTER NINETEEN

PUBLIC SPEAKING

Master the Benefits of Public Speaking
Speak for Success

INTRODUCTION

Do you have public speaking skills? Are you comfortable speaking to small or large groups of people?

Public speaking is a skill every professional should possess. Are you comfortable speaking in public? Public speaking is one of the most important in-demand soft skills and considered the biggest professional and social fear. This essential core competency is expected and required in the new workplace. To be successful depends on your ability to effectively communicate.

What are the advantages of public speaking skills?

Public speaking has unique career advantages to speak with confidence for interviews, promotions, interpersonal communication, negotiation, and deal with difficult behavior, present ideas, products, services and other workplace and social situations.

Public speaking is a transferable skill used to increase your marketability to employers, enhance your communication skills, focus your message and organize your thoughts.

What are the disadvantages of not acquiring public speaking skills?

Professionals who do not possess this valuable soft skill can limit employment, and advancement opportunities, the ability to effectively communicate with management, colleagues, customers, clients and others. Listed are ways to learn public speaking skills.

Master public speaking skills by:
- Join a professional speaking organization which teaches speaking and leadership skills.
- Volunteer to give small informal group presentations until you gain the confidence to speak to larger and formal groups.

What are the long-term benefits of mastering public speaking skills?

Public speaking skills enable you to:
- Effectively communicate to individuals and groups.
- Improve relationships.
- Make presentations.
- Build self confidence.
- Influence others.
- Put you on the fast track to career and personal success.

Listed are public speaking skills benefits to excel in your career.

Fifteen Benefits to Speak for Success

1. **Audience.** Allows you to interact and understand the needs of the audience.
2. **Confidence.** Helps you improve self confidence and communication skills.
3. **Creates Messages.** Helps you create informative messages that are appropriate for audiences.
4. **Critical Thinking Skills.** Improves your ability to communicate, identify and analyze problem solving solutions.
5. **Difficult Behavior.** Provides speaking skills to manage relations with difficult behavior and bully type personalities.
6. **Influences.** Allows you to influence others with your ideas.
7. **Interpersonal Skills.** Improves your interactions and ability to engage others in a conversation.
8. **Interviews.** Increase your marketability to employers.
9. **Listening Skills.** Improves active listening skills.
10. **New Professional Opportunities.** Opens the door and increases new professional opportunities.
11. **New Social Opportunities.** Increase social opportunities to meet others and build strategic relationships.
12. **Organizational Skills.** Helps you organize, present and communicate your thoughts.
13. **Presentation Skills.** Improve your presentation skills.
14. **Self Expression.** Effectively express your ideas, beliefs, values and opinions to others.
15. **Visibility.** Increase visibility with management,

executives and competitors for career advancement. Increase visibility in social, professional organizations and your brand community.

To be successful at work depends on our ability to communicate effectively. Public speaking skills are no longer a career option in the workplace. In the new workplace public speaking is a required skill for all professionals.

Summary

Public Speaking

Key Points:
Public speaking is an in-demand marketable skill and valuable career asset which can help you:

- Master the benefits of public speaking.
- Gain recognition and respect from management and peers.
- Improve your self confidence.
- Improve your marketability for employment and financial rewards.
- Build your reputation and increase professional and social visibility.
- Build strong strategic relationships.
- Influence and motivate others.
- Promote your company and its products and services.

CHAPTER TWENTY

RISK TAKING

Are You A Risk Taker?
How to Take Risks and Get Ahead at Work

INTRODUCTION

Do you take risks at work?

Risk taking is a growing and important skill in the workplace. Organizations accept new projects and promote employees to positions where there is increased responsibility. These new roles require employees to execute projects, take risks and be accountable for the results.

Three Types of Risks Probability

Type 1: Low Risk Probability
- Low level risk – very little risk or importance.

Type 2: Medium Risk Probability
- Medium risks are of moderate importance – these are risks you can manage and move on.

Type 3: High Risk Probability – Contingency Plan
- High risks are of importance – these risks could happen and will need immediate attention if they happen.
- High risks will require a contingency plan to be in place.

To manage project risks – focus on individual strategies for high priority risks which are the most critical and medium risks which are manageable.

Risk Management: Seven Ways to Manage Risks

1. Ask for What You Want
- You have a greater chance of getting what you want when you ask for it.

2. Do Not Risk Everything
- Do not risk everything if it will ruin you emotionally, financially, physically or your career.

3. Positive Risks
- The risks you take should not put you or others at risk – or involve emotional or physical harm.

4. Turn Failure to Success
- Identify risk failures and learn from the experience.
- Apply what you have learned to your next risk.

5. Risk Taking
- The more risks you take the more confident you will feel about risk taking.
- Start with small risks and progress based on how it will impact you.

6. Identify What You Want
- Move forward with what you want even though others might not be in agreement.

7. Take Risks
- If you have nothing to lose always take the risk.

Risk Taking: Six Types of Risk Taking to Avoid

Type 1: What You Will Lose
- There is a good chance you will lose everything.

Type 2: On the Line
- Your risk is greater than your return.

Type 3: Uncontrollable Factors
- There are multiple factors which you cannot control.

Type 4: What Are the Odds?
- When your instincts tell you the odds are not in your favor.

Type 5: Outcome
- There is no way to reverse the outcome if it does not turn out the way you want.

Type 6: Preparation
- You are faced with a risk where there is no time to prepare or evaluate the risk.

Taking a first risk will build confidence and preparation for future risks. In order to get what you want and be successful there will always be risks.

Risk Taking: Five Benefits to Risk Taking

Each person's risk tolerance changes over time. A risk worth taking by one person may not be worth it for another – risk taking is unique to each person. Listed are the benefits of risk taking.

1. Overcome Fears
- Overcome fear of risk taking by facing smaller risks then bigger risks.

2. No Risk – No Reward
- If you do not take risks you will not have the chance to experience the rewards.

3. Awareness
- Awareness of potential risks and loss provides an appreciation for what is at risk.

4. Challenges
- Risk provides challenges to learn and strengthen your ability to face and overcome fear.

5. Focus
- The ability to focus, control, manage and overcome fears helps you manage risk in other areas of your life.

Summary

Risk Taking

Key Points:

- Whether you accept a new project with risk probability or take responsibility of a new promotion – both involve taking risks.
- Risk taking is expected in business – some people are better at it than others.
- Some professionals who gain more experience tend to take fewer risks – possibly they have more to lose.
- When you stop taking risks you limit your career opportunities.
- The decision to take risks is unique to each person.
- Ask for what you want is one way of managing risks.
- "Uncontrollable factors" is one type of risk taking to avoid.
- When the odds are not in your favor avoid the risk.
- Awareness is one of the benefits of risk taking.
- Awareness of a potential risk and loss provides an appreciation for what is at risk.
- Where there is *no risk* – there is *no reward*.

"When you believe in yourself –
there are no limits to what you can achieve."

\- PATRICIA DORCH

CHAPTER TWENTY ONE

SELF CONFIDENCE

Self Confidence
Thirteen Steps to Build Self Confidence

INTRODUCTION

Are you self confident? Are you afraid to speak up at meetings for concern others might not agree with your input? Do you have good posture?

Self confidence is the difference between feeling confident or unsure about yourself. How you see yourself will impact how others see you – perception is everything. The way you feel about yourself has an impact how others perceive and treat you. The more self confidence you have the more successful you will be.

During an interview an employer will quickly access whether you are a confident person.

Self confidence impacts every area of your work life. These steps will enable you to become self confident and successful.

Thirteen Steps to Build Self Confidence

Step 1: Be Grateful
- Focus on gratitude.
- Make a list of what you have to be grateful.
- Recall past success.
- Identify unique skills.
- Identify successful relationships.

Step 2: Circle of Influence:
- Associate with people who have the same goals and ambition instead of the same problems.

Step 3: Compliments
- Break the cycle of thinking negatively about yourself.
- Graciously accept compliments about yourself rather than making excuses.
- Get in the habit of complimenting others.
- Refuse to engage in gossip.
- Look for the best in others – and bring out the best in yourself.

Step 4: Dress for Success
- When you look good you feel good.
- Use your positive image as an advantage when you interact with others.
- Wear clean and up to date clothing and polish your grooming.

Step 5: Exercise
- If you are out of shape you feel less energetic, insecure and unattractive.
- Physical fitness has an impact on self confidence.
- Working out improves physical appearance and provides energy.

Step 6: Feel Good About Yourself
- Identify what you do well.

Step 7: Good Posture
- People with poor posture communicate a lack of self confidence.
- Good posture communicates confidence when you stand straight, make good eye contact and hold your head up.

Step 8: Make A Contribution
- Stop thinking about yourself.
- Make a contribution to the world, and be rewarded with career and personal success and recognition.

Step 9: Personal Pitch
- Listen to and attend motivational seminars.
- Write a 30-60 second pitch about your achievements, strengths and goals.
- Recite your accomplishments out loud to boost your confidence.

Step 10: Positive Self-Talk
- Keep your self-talk positive.
- Look for the good in you – count the things that are positive not negative.

Step 11: Sit Up Front

- At work, meetings, conferences and activities sit up front and be noticed.
- Sitting up front builds your confidence.
- Sitting up front allows you to be more visible to important people who talk in front of the room.

Step 12: Speak Up

- Speaking up builds your confidence and public speaking skills.
- Speaking up will position you to be recognized as a leader.

Step 13: Walk Faster

Do you walk slowly? Do you show a lack of enthusiasm? Does your pace show a lack of energy?

- Walk with purpose and energy.
- People who are confident walk quickly – they have places to go, people to see and goals to accomplish.
- Walking faster will make you feel and look more confident.

Summary

Self Confidence

Key Points:

- How you see yourself will impact how others see you.
- A positive appearance is an advantage when you interact with others.

- Walk faster with confidence, purpose and energy.
- Positive body language will make you feel more empowered.
- You are more visible in meetings and conferences when you sit up front.
- Speaking up at meetings and conferences builds your confidence.
- Good posture communicates confidence.
- Compliment others – break the cycle of thinking negatively about yourself.

CHAPTER TWENTY TWO

SELF MOTIVATION

Self Motivation
Motivate Yourself to Accomplish Goals

INTRODUCTION

Are you motivated to achieve goals? How do you motivate yourself to meet your obligations?

It may be easy to sit back and watch deadlines for college, or work go unaccomplished. Whether you are at college or in the workplace you will need to motivate yourself to complete assignments, reports and other tasks. Listed are tips to help you motivate yourself to accomplish goals.

Eleven Smart Tips to Get Motivated

Tip 1: Set Specific Goals
- Set definite specific goals.

Tip 2: Challenge
- Select goals that are challenging.

Tip 3: Visualize
- Visualizing your goals will motivate you.

Tip 4: Small Goals
- Start with small daily goals you want to achieve.

Tip 5: Pace Yourself
- Pace yourself to accomplish each goal.

Tip 6: Believe in Yourself
- Believe in yourself and gain confidence to achieve goals.

Tip 7: Be Responsible
- Prove yourself by being responsible.

Tip 8: Reward Yourself
- Reward yourself for completing your goals.

Tip 9: Do Not Give Up
- Do not give up if you need more time than planned to achieve your goal.

Tip 10: Organize Your Time
- Organize your time and environment.

Tip 11: Past Achievements
- Identify what motivated you to achieve past achievements and use the success to motivate you to achieve future goals.

Summary

Self Motivation

Key Points:
- Set definite specific goals.
- Start with small daily goals you want to achieve.
- Believe in yourself to accomplish goals.
- Be responsible – achieve goals you have set.
- Do not give up – focus on the desired outcome.

CHAPTER TWENTY THREE

TIME MANAGEMENT

Time Management
How to Increase Workplace Productivity

INTRODUCTION

Do you know how to manage your time? Are you productive with the time allowed to accomplished workplace goals?

There is pressure in the workplace to get more things done and be productive. To increase workplace productivity become more efficient with your time. Establishing your relationship with time is an important part of learning to use time more efficiently. Everyone's relationship with time is different; therefore managing time will vary accordingly.

Your strengths, weaknesses, commitments, lifestyles, and workplace responsibilities all plays a role in your time management system. Learn how to manage time and tasks by using the following tools.

Fourteen Tools to Help You Be Productive

Tool 1: Deadlines
- Take deadlines to complete assignments seriously.
- Scheduling deadlines gives you direction and confirms your commitment to meet deadlines.
- Plan time in your calendar to review and accomplish deadlines.
- Do not wait until the day before a deadline occurs to work on an assignment – planning ahead allows time for unforeseen circumstances that could interfere with meeting deadlines.
- Personal excuses other than family emergencies are not acceptable in the workplace.

Tool 2: Email
- Do not check your email 100 times per day.
- Check your email a few times in the morning, mid-day, a few times in the afternoon and at the end of the day.

Tool 3: Meeting Management
- Be on time for *all* meetings, seminars, conferences, teleconferences and webinars.
- Do not schedule back to back meetings – most meetings usually run late.

Tool 4: Faulty-Tasking
- Do not over multi-task.
- Over multi-tasking leads to faulty- tasking - more tasks started and less things done.

Tool 5: Organization
- Stay organized.
- Disorganization leads to wasting valuable time.

Tool 6: Stop Answering the Phone
- Do not answer the phone when you are in the presence of other people.
- Do not answer the phone when you are in the middle of a project that has a deadline.
- Screen phone calls to determine which messages require immediate attention and others that can wait for a better time.
- Let your messages go to voice mail except if you are expecting an important phone call.

Tool 7: Task Management Tools

New Tasks
- Allocate enough time for new tasks.
- New tasks may take two times longer than tasks you are familiar.

Make a List
- Write down your tasks.
- Put your list in front of you.

Day List
- Make a list of tasks to be completed on a specific day.

This Week
- Make a list of tasks to be completed this week.

Thirty Days
- Make a list of tasks to be completed in the next thirty days.

Task Schedule - Planning
- **Appointments.** Schedule appointments with your tasks.
- **Activities.** Schedule important activities such as teleconferences, webinars, meetings, appointments, due dates, and deadlines – add them to your calendar.
- **Calendar.** Use a monthly calendar with weekly goals to achieve. Your monthly calendar or notebook is a time-saving device. Consistent use of a calendar provides a visual reminder of your commitments.
- **Dates.** Highlight important dates and reports on your calendar in color.

Tool 8: The Power of One
- Keep things simple.
- Do not have too many tools in your tool kit – downsize to use one tool with multiple options.

Tool 9: Things to Do List – Visible
- Keep your "things to do list" visible so you will know your accomplishments throughout the day.

Tool 10: Unplug
- Unplug from your devices to allow time to mentally regroup.

Tool 11: Set Priorities
- Identify work priorities.
- Write down your priorities; be specific as possible.
- Rank the importance of multiple priorities.
- Too many priorities at the same time will increase stress.

Tool 12: Goals
- **Translate.** Translate your priorities into goals.

- **Activities.** Break each goal into activities and identify the steps required to achieve the goal.
- **Resources.** Identify resources needed to accomplish your goal; you might require the assistance of other people.

Tool 13: Personal Time Management Barriers
- Do you feel "too controlled?"
- Is the task you need to accomplish boring?
- Identify your own barriers to effective time management.

Tool 14: Achieve "Meaningful" Outcomes
- Effective time management will assist you in achieving meaningful outcomes, not more outcomes.

Summary

Time Management

Key Points:
- To increase workplace productivity become more efficient with your time.
- Take deadlines seriously.
- Be on time for all meetings, conferences, teleconferences, seminars and webinars.
- Do not over multi-task.
- New tasks may take two times longer than tasks you are familiar.
- Schedule appointments for your tasks.
- Highlight in color important due dates on your calendar.
- Unapproved excuses for not meeting deadlines is not acceptable in the workplace.

- Keep your things do list visible throughout the day.
- Unplug from your devices to allow time to regroup.
- Identify your own personal time management barriers and how to overcome them.
- Achieve more meaningful outcomes not more outcomes.

"Networking is building relationships, help others and giving advice to anyone who asks."
-PATRICIA DORCH

CHAPTER TWENTY FOUR

HOW TO NETWORK

How To Network
Seventeen Essential Business Strategies
for the 21st Century

INTRODUCTION

Do you know how to network? Do you know how to build internal and external business relationships? Do you know the process of what business networking entails?

What is Networking?

Effective networking strategies provide access to knowledge, expertise, and allies to support you both professionally and personally. Networking requires a mission, goals, vision, and a willingness to share valuable information with others. Networking events are places to make plans to meet new contacts, reconnect and stay in contact with others.

Networking is building relationships, help others and giving advice to anyone who asks. A trusting professional or personal relationship will enhance your base of internal and external contacts and build a lifetime of rewards. Listed are networking strategies to enhance your business networking skills.

How to N.E.T.W.O.R.K

Names – Remember people's names.

Eye – Eye contact is important.

Talk – Talk, but also listen to what is being said.

Write – Write follow-up notes on a regular basis.

Open – Be open and ask questions.

Resource – Become a resource for others.

Knowledge – Knowledge is the ability to control your future.

STRATEGY 1:
INTRODUCTIONS AND MARKETING
STATEMENT ("ELEVATOR SPEECH")

First Impressions
- Make positive first impressions with business associates and colleagues.

Three Tips for Introductions
1. Make eye contact and extend a confident handshake.
2. Eliminate trendy words such as "cool" and "awesome" from your vocabulary in a business environment.
3. Carry company or personal professional materials which represent your organization such as pens, note pads, a computer bag and others. These items are a positive reflection of your professional style.

The Proper Handshake
The purpose of a handshake is to establish rapport and positive chemistry between two people. A handshake is a form of non-verbal communication. It's appropriate to shake hands in a business setting. Gender does not determine whether to shake hands or not.

Your handshake communicates:
- Professionalism
- Confidence
- Credibility

When to Stand

It is proper to stand when shaking hands during introductions unless you are seated in an environment such as a restaurant that makes standing difficult. Standing balances the power between you and your contact. The person standing is presumed to have the power.

A firm handshake conveys:
- Assurance
- Confidence
- Interest
- Respect

The Name Game

Everyone likes to have his or her name remembered, pronounced, and spelled correctly. Making an effort to remember names strengthens personal and business relationships.

Six techniques to help you remember names:

1. **Listen** – Listen carefully to people's names.
2. **Repeat.** If you are not sure you heard the person's name correctly, or if you did not understand what the person said, ask them to repeat the name.
3. **Reinforcement.** Repeat the name back to the person for reinforcement and confirmation only if you did not understand.
4. **Syllables.** Break the name down into syllables for yourself.
5. **Connection.** Connect the name with something familiar to you.
6. **Unique.** Identify something unique about the person and their name.

Marketing Statement (Also known as "Elevator Speech or Introduction")

Your marketing statement should be something about yourself that engages people in a conversation. Tailor your marketing statement to the event. It should be:

- **Planned** – Write down what you want to say prior to the event.
- **Practiced** – Rehearse out loud prior to the event to hear how you sound.
- **Succinct** – Make sure you pronounce your words clearly.
- **Interesting** – Use appropriate humor to create interest in your introduction.

Example:

Hello, my name is Richard King from sunny San Diego, California. I'm attending the annual International New Technology Conference.

STRATEGY 2: BUSINESS IMAGE TIPS

Make a Power Statement –Show You Mean Business!

Dressing appropriately for business in the 21st Century is an essential element of doing business. Never underestimate the power of first impressions. It takes less than ten seconds for someone to form an impression of you based on what they see.

In business, power and credibility are based on people's perception of you. Position yourself where you want to go professionally; your clothing sends a message how serious you are. Ask yourself, "How do I look?" What you wear today could impact your career tomorrow.

Appearances Do Count!

Appearance is based on the following percentages and characteristics.

- **55%** - Appearance and body language.
- **38%** - Vocal tone, pacing, and voice inflection.
- **7%** - Verbal message.

Power Image Career Opportunities

- You never know who is observing your appearance.
- Position your image for promotions.
- Dress for your *next* position.
- Think about the perception others might have of your non-verbal communication.
- Consider the positive or negative impact your image may have on your career and future.
- Make business decisions.

STRATEGY 3: HOW TO DEFINE YOUR NETWORKING GOALS

Write specific long and short-term goals.

What are your goals?

- **Immediate:** Three to six months.
- **Short-term:** Nine to twelve months.
- **Long-term:** One to five years.

Why are these goals important to you?

- Have you made the commitment to achieve these goals?

Who are the people I need to help me?

- How can I recruit them?
- How can they help me?

When can I expect to achieve my goals?

- How will I know when I have achieved them?

STRATEGY 4: INFORMATION, INFLUENCE, RESOURCES AND VOLUNTEER

Know what you have to offer and what you have to gain.

Information

Seek information relative to your job search or business needs. Use social media resources to assist you in your search.

Influence

- Define a strategy to meet and network with new people.
- Position yourself to have access to key people.
- Identify people who have the ability to connect you to what you need to achieve your goal.

Resources

- Know where to go. Ask questions if you need assistance.
- Make reasonable requests from your network.
- Do not ask for more than a person can afford to give.
- Be considerate of your contact's position and yours.
- Become a resource for others.

Volunteer

- Volunteer for career and business projects.
- Build relationships while helping a personal, professional, or business cause.
- Volunteer work gives you the opportunity to get involved and show your skills to potential future business contacts.

STRATEGY 5: HOW TO EXCHANGE BUSINESS CARDS

Effective business card exchange occurs when your contact can become a resource for you or others you know.

Exchanging business cards with someone does not constitute a networking relationship. Challenge yourself not to give out your cards, until you have uncovered a reason for exchanging names and phone numbers.

Lead your conversation in a direction that may be beneficial for you and your contact to exchange business cards beyond the event purpose.

Business Card Exchange Tips

Read your contact's business card carefully – ask questions about information on the card. Asking questions shows interest in your contact and a great way to start a conversation.

- **Business Cards.** Bring enough business cards.
- **Date the Card.** Put the date on the front top right corner of the business card; put the event or occasion and additional notes on the back of the card as a reference.
- **Card System.** Devise a personal system for exchanging your cards with your contacts.
- **Unique.** Ask about unique spellings of an individual or a company name.
- **Achievements.** Ask about initials, degrees, and certifications.
- **Ask Questions.** Ask questions about industries which you have little or no knowledge.
- **Clarify Status.** Clarify whether the person works for a company or is an entrepreneur.

Networking Signature Tools

- **Custom Name Badge** – Invest in a custom prepared name badge. Put your name, company name, or field of interest or title on the name badge.
- **Name Badge.** Wear your name badge on the right side, this will ensure your name is clearly seen when you shake hands.
- **Quality Pen and Pencil Set.** Purchase a quality brand pen and pencil set, or have others give them to you as a gift on your birthday, graduation or special occasion. Use black ink for business. Engraving your name is a nice touch for professional branding. *Inform the engraver if you are left handed.*

- **Quality Business Cards**. Invest in quality printed business cards. Do not use a service which prints "free" on the reverse side - this takes away from your professional image.
- **Professional Business Tools.** Use a leather writing portfolio or electronic device. Always be prepared to take notes. Use a leather writing portfolio that will accommodate a notepad which has pockets to store your business cards and those you collect.

STRATEGY 6: HOW TO MANAGE YOUR CONTACTS

Make time to keep in touch.

After a networking event, sort through business cards to determine which ones you need, and follow up with those contacts within three business days.

Develop a system to manage your contacts by using these four tool options.

- **Software.** Use electronic contact management software.
- **Mobile Device.** Use a contact management system that is mobile.
- **Electronic Filing System.** Use a business card electronic filing system.
- **Manual Filing System.** Use a three-ring notebook with plastic business card holders to file your business cards.

STRATEGY 7: HOW TO MAKE SMALL CONVERSATIONS

Small conversations are an effective way to learn about each other.

Use your experience and environment to create conversations about business, career, sports, lifestyle, and other topics that will help others feel comfortable with you.

Key 1: Media

- Listen to world news or read the newspaper or internet daily.

Key 2: Topics

- Avoid sensitive topics such as sex, religion, and politics unless you are attending a function involving these topics.

Key 3: Read

- Read books, newsletters, professional journals, blogs and business magazines.

Key 4: Notes

- Take notes about important information for your networking goals.

Key 5: Humor

- Use humor in good taste and avoid sexist and racial comments.

Key 6: Listen

- Listen actively.

Key 7: New Opportunities

- Say YES to new business and professional opportunities!

STRATEGY 8: HOW TO ENGAGE YOUR CONNECTION

Make a commitment to learn public speaking skills. Listen and observe speaking styles of others you admire and want to incorporate with your personal style.

The letters in the word "engage" will help you remember the process of engaging your connection in a conversation.

E ye – Establish and maintain good eye contact.

N od – Nod to encourage communication.

G reet – Greet people with a friendly smile, hello, and handshake.

A ttention – Focus your attention on what is being said.

G esturing – Gesturing your hands when you talk enhances your message.

E ase – Be at ease and comfortable with your connection.

STRATEGY 9: HOW TO CLOSE THE CONVERSATION

Six Strategies to Close the Conversation: Closing Statements

Use closing statements that will help you transition to your next contact. When you leave gracefully, you leave the door open to reconnect at another time.

Would you excuse me?

1. I want to meet the host.
2. I want to meet the speaker.
3. I promised to meet with a few colleagues before they leave.
4. I'm going to meet new potential clients.
5. I want to say hello to an existing client.
6. I do not want to take your networking time.

L.E.A.V.E Technique

L et go of your contact after five minutes to work the event.

E xplain why you are there and find out why your connection is there.

A ct on your planned agenda.

V isualize your next move.

E xit gracefully after shaking hands.

STRATEGY 10: HOW TO LISTEN

1. Focus on the speaker.
2. Listen to understand from the speaker's perspective.
3. Maintain good eye contact.
4. Ask questions and provide feedback that demonstrates your interest.
5. Observe others body language.
6. Identify and acknowledge mutual interests.
7. Keep an open mind and take mental and written notes. When you identify - you have something to offer, the next step is to exchange business cards, ideas, resources, and referrals. Show your competence in what you say and do. Always respect confidentiality and support the success of your contact.

STRATEGY 11: HOW TO WORK THE ROOM

Plan Your Presence

- **Listener.** Be a good listener and encourage others to share information. When people talk about themselves you find out about them and their business.
- **Goal.** Work the room with a goal in mind.
- **Manage your time.** Do not spend the entire time with one person.
- **Limit.** Limit the amount of time you spend with people you know.
- **Manners.** Be kind to everyone!
- **Be open to all people**. Do not judge others based on physical appearances, disabilities, and culture – be open to all people.
- **Judgment**. Use good business judgment.

- **Questions.** Ask the right questions and gather valuable information.
- **What you have in common.** Focus on what you have in common – the event.
- **Body language.** Be aware of body language. When two people are face-to-face, they usually do not want to be interrupted. If they are standing side-by-side, it's more likely you are welcomed to join the conversation.
- **Ask permission.** Ask permission to join a group of three or more. Never interrupt or change the subject they are discussing; wait for a break in the conversation.
- **Comments.** Limit your comments to three to five minutes and invite feedback from others.

STRATEGY 12: HOW TO BUILD TRUST

Teach Your Contacts About Your Character

Contacts must see you in action to observe your behavior or hear favorable comments about you from others. If you make a commitment to do something - follow it through.

Listed are ten guidelines to help teach contacts about your character.

1. **Be reliable.**
2. **Deadlines.** Meet deadlines and commitments.
3. **Solutions.** Create win-win solutions.
4. **Respect.** Treat everyone with respect.
5. **Speak positively.** Speak positively about all people.
6. **Collaborate.** Collaborate with others rather than compete.
7. **Correct.** Correct mistakes and apologize.

8. **Go the extra mile.** Go the extra mile – do more than what is expected.
9. **Respect.** Respect other people's time and privacy.
10. **Compensate.** Compensate for failures – offer to volunteer your services or help someone who might need you assistance.

STRATEGY 13: POWER ETIQUETTE AND MANNERS

Good manners can open doors that money, position and power cannot.

Power Etiquette

How you relate to others is what etiquette is all about. Your attitude is a personality trait developed throughout your life. Understand the power of your attitude; it impacts everything you do.

Signs of Your Attitude

- Your body language.
- How you take care of yourself.
- How you complete your assignments.
- Your attention to detail.

Good Manners in Business

Good manners can open doors that money, position, and power cannot.

- Respect the organizations culture.
- Treat rank with respect.

- Respect others and their privacy.
- Be courteous to everyone.

Cell Phone and Other Electronic Devices

Use good business judgment. Turn off electronic devices prior to:

- Networking functions.
- All business-related functions.

Use a vibration option to alert you of messages.

- Do not answer your phone or other electronic device in the presence of others.
- Leave the networking event area to respond to phone calls, send or check messages.
- When you look at your electronic devices, your contact will think you need to leave the conversation.
- Gracefully exit before leaving to respond to an alert.

STRATEGY 14: HOW TO FOLLOW-UP

Visibility is valuable.

Build Relationships: R.E.A.C.H. Technique

Effective follow-up is the most important step in the networking process. Often, people invest their time, energy, and money to attend functions and make contacts, but spend little or no time in building relationships with others. Following up and keeping in touch are essential for successful networking.

Relationships – Build relationships with networking contacts.

Engage – Engage contacts in a meaningful conversation.

Action – Take action based on your outcome.

Contact – Contact referrals instrumental to your success.

How – Ask how you can become a resource for others.

STRATEGY 15: HOW TO NETWORK AT WORK

"Networking in the 21ˢᵗ century is more important for your career than every before."

-PATRICIA DORCH

Win Inside

No matter where you work – a government agency, a corporation, a non-profit organization, or an association – networking is more important to your career than ever before.

Traditional career paths are rapidly changing. People must rely on their ability to build networks at work and manage their careers. Social networking is a preferred alternative to traditional organizational charts and everyday business transactions.

A network of contacts – both inside and outside of an organization – is the most important thing a professional can do for their careers. To get hired or promoted spend time networking.

It's Not Who You Know…It's Who Knows You!

Why Network at Work?

Change – Use your network to stay informed about organizational change.

Bottom Line – You job depends on the success of the organization.

Venture – Step out into non-traditional career opportunities.

Collaboration – Increase teamwork with other people and departments.

Expand Your Knowledge – Create a network of people with different interests and expertise.

Networking Benefits

- **Increase visibility.** New opportunities will find you.
- **Accountability and responsibility.** Manage your "own" career.
- **Options.** Always keep your career and business options open.

Transferable Skills

- Determine a strategy to showcase your knowledge, skills, abilities, and interest to others.

Networking Thoughts

- What resources do you have to help others?
- What can you offer others in your networking relationship?

Where to Network

- Bulletin Boards
- Circulation Lists
- e-networks
- Formal or informal networks
- Mailing Lists
- Virtual Communities

STRATEGY 16: NETWORKING ORGANIZATIONS

Networking with people will bring you a world of opportunities.

- **Visibility.** Visibility is valuable. Make the most of your time.
- **Arrival Time.** Arrive early, stay late, and meet the movers and shakers.
- **Make Conversations.** Make conversations about your career, business goals, or other objectives.
- **Resource.** Become a resource for others.

Professional Networks

- Advisory Boards
- Associations
- Committees
- Government Agencies
- Inter-Agency Groups

- Organizations
- Project Specific Groups
- Suppliers
- Work Teams
- Others

STRATEGY 17: HOW TO NETWORK AS A WAY OF LIFE

Networking has a beginning but no end.

Networking will bring you personal and professional success. Make the most of your time; be determined, patient, and visible.

Practice conversations with people in familiar and uncommon places. Asking questions is a sign of a good listener and will help you establish rapport and build relationships. Networking has a beginning and no end.

Summary

How to Network

Key Points:
- Networking is building relationships, helping others and giving advice to anyone who asks.
- Effective networking strategies provide access to knowledge and expertise.
- A handshake communicates – professionalism, confidence and credibility.

- Dressing appropriately for business in the 21st Century is an essential element of doing business.
- Effective business card exchange occurs when your contact can become a resource for you or others you know.
- Make a commitment to learn public speaking skills.
- Be a good listener and encourage others to share information.
- Effective follow-up is the most important step in the networking process.
- A network of contacts – both inside and outside of an organization – is the most important thing a professional can do for their career.
- Networking will bring you personal and professional success. Make the most of your time; be determined, patient, and visible.
- Networking has a beginning and no end.

CHAPTER TWENTY FIVE

TECHNOLOGY

Technology Skills

Technology literacy applies to all levels of employees in the workplace from entry level, highly skilled, management, supervisors and executives. To be able to use the computer, internet and other technology are necessary for all professionals to do their job.

Organizations rely heavily on computers and the internet to complete day to day tasks. Technology competency is a valuable and important business tool. Technology skills depending on the job requirements may be considered both soft and hard skills – therefore computer skills are important to meet the job demands.

"Soft skills enhance your marketability for career success."
-PATRICIA DORCH

SOFT SKILLS FOR CAREER SUCCESS

Soft skills are essential for employment, management and leadership positions.

Oral and written communication skills are important to get hired and promoted.

Flexibility allows you to easily adapt to the work environment, new ideas and work habits.

Teamwork skills require active participants who listen, speak up, and take the initiative to make things happen.

Strong work ethic is critical to achieve organizational goals.

Knowledge is needed to perform the required tasks in the workplace.

Interpersonal communication skills are essential in every area of your life.

Listening skills increases your ability to influence, increase productivity, effectively negotiate and reduce misunderstandings.

Leadership skills empower you to lead instead of manage your team.

Speaking skills builds self confidence and increases your value in the workplace.

WHAT ARE
SOFT**SKILLS**?

How to Master Essential Skills to Achieve
Workplace Success

Summary

Whether you are a college student, intern, college graduate, working professional or returning to the workforce soft skills are crucial to your success in the workplace.

Today organizations provide far less training for soft skills; therefore job candidates need to acquire these essential employability skills. To get the best jobs and stand out from the competition job candidates are expected to take ownership and the initiative to learn soft skills. These skills prepare you to meet the changing requirements and demands to get hired and promoted.

What Are Soft Skills? How to Master Essential Skills to Achieve Workplace Success will prepare you for the new workplace and your roadmap to thrive in any organization and economy.

ABOUT THE AUTHOR

PATRICIA DORCH is President and CEO OF EXECU DRESS. She has a Master of Science in Business Organizational Management from the University of LaVerne in LaVerne, CA. Patricia has a background in outside Sales and Marketing for major business, medical, healthcare and pharmaceutical corporations.

Patricia is the author of *Professionalism: New Rules for Workplace Career Success, Job Search: College Graduates New Career Advice, Ideas and Strategies to Get Hired, Military To Civilian Transition: Job Search Strategies and Tips to Get Hired in the Civilian Job Market, Job Search: New Get Hired Ideas, Tips and Strategies for 40 Plus, Six Figure Career Coaching Advice: The Ultimate Guide to Achieving Success, Job Search: Teen Interview Tips and Strategies to Get Hired and What Are Soft Skills? How to Master Essential Skills to Achieve Workplace Success.*

Patricia is an in-demand speaker, career expert and article contributor who specializes in maximizing the potential for professionals to get hired, demonstrate professionalism in the workplace and get promoted in today's ultra competitive job market.

Are you looking for a speaker? Patricia is a dynamic speaker and trainer – schedule her for your next speaker program, conference, meeting, regional or local training, job or career fair, career day or other event at:

Website: www.whataresoftskills.net
Email: Patricia@whataresoftskills.net

WHAT ARE
SOFTSKILLS?

How to Master Essential Skills to Achieve Workplace Success

PATRICIA DORCH

Job Search

New
Get Hired
Ideas, Tips and
Strategies for
40 Plus

PATRICIA DORCH

SIX FIGURE
CAREER
COACHING
ADVICE

PATRICIA DORCH

THE ULTIMATE GUIDE
TO ACHIEVING SUCCESS

MILITARY TO CIVILIAN TRANSITION
JOB
Search Strategies
and Tips to GET HIRED in the
CIVILIAN JOB MARKET

PATRICIA DORCH

JOB SEARCH

COLLEGE GRADUATES

New Career Advice, Ideas and Strategies
TO GET HIRED

PATRICIA DORCH

PRO·FES·SION·AL·ISM

Professionalism
New Rules
for Workplace
Career Success

PATRICIA DORCH

WHAT ARE
SOFTSKILLS?

How to Master Essential Skills to Achieve Workplace Success

PATRICIA DORCH

www.ingramcontent.com/pod-product-compliance
Lightning Source LLC
LaVergne TN
LVHW051521080426
835509LV00017B/2140